WILD About Northeastern Birds

A Youth's Guide

by Adele Porter

Adventure Publications, Inc.
Cambridge, Minnesota

This book is dedicated to Byron, Elizabeth and Rachael. Wamlati!

This book is also dedicated to my sister, an enthusiastic Northeasterner.

To the children of the Northeast, may your wildest wishes come true.

Acknowledgments

Carrol Henderson, Minnesota DNR Nongame Wildlife Program:

Thank you for your continued support and for allowing the use of your photographs of the Handsaker Egg Collection.

Orville and Mary Telford and Roland and Anna Bernau, keepers of the land:

Thank you for your friendship, inspiration and for providing living land museums to explore.

Friends, the neighborhood team, and the teachers and students that shared their ideas and support:

Thank you for your invaluable enthusiasm and input.

Joan Galli, Wildlife Biologist, Nongame Wildlife Specialist

Thank you for your review of the book and for sharing your in-depth knowledge of the lands and birds of the Northeastern United States.

Emily C., neighbor extraordinaire:

Thank you for sharing your engaging journal notes on the American Robin!

The numerous staff members of the conservation and natural resource departments of the ten states represented in this book that willingly provided data, background and supporting facts.

Thank you for your dedication to the stewardship of natural resources and for your willingness to share your knowledge, skills and enthusiasm.

My sincere thanks to the countless professionals and volunteers that have contributed their time, energy and field data to state and federal reports, breeding-bird atlases, bird counts and other citizen science projects. The collaborative efforts of wildlife professionals and volunteers across North America, as well as globally important migratory wintering areas, provide vital information to the life histories and population status of birds. These resources have been imperative to the writing of *Wild About Northeastern Birds*.

Edited by Gretchen Jensen, Anthony Hertzel and Brett Ortler

Book and cover design, nest, migration map and habitat map illustrations by Jonathan Norberg

Habitat Café, feather, exterior and interior of bird illustrations by Julie Martinez; range maps and bird silhouette illustrations by Anthony Hertzel; cartoon bird illustrations by Brenna Slabaugh; child's nest drawing by Emily Connick

Photo credits by photographer and page number:

Egg photos: Chester A. Reed, *North American Birds Eggs*: 43 **R. L. Ridgway, *Life Histories of North American Birds*:** 49, 145 all other egg photos from the Handsaker Egg Collection taken by Carrol Henderson

Rick and Nora Bowers: 140 (main) **Dudley Edmondson:** 42 (female), 142 (soaring), 144 (both) **John Gerlach/DPA*:** 32 (main) **Carrol Henderson:** 156 (winter), 180 (gosling) **Adele Porter:** 108 (Canada anemone) **Johann Schumacher/CLO*:** 162 (female) **Brian E. Small:** 64 (female), 130 (main), 172 (winter) **Alan Stankevitz:** 6 (Great Blue Heron, Barred Owl), 8 (American Oystercatcher), 44 (both), 46 (fanned tail), 62, 70, 72 (female), 74, 84, 86 (juvenile), 94 (both), 96, 98 (main), 102 (spitting pellet), 112 (main), 114, 116, 120 (in flight), 122 (both), 124 (main), 126 (both), 132 (both), 134, 138 (in flight), 152 (both), 160, 166 (female), 170, 176 (in flight), 182 (in flight), 184 (feeding), 186 (in flight) **Stan Tekiela:** 6 (Eastern Bluebird), 7 (Mallard, Indigo Bunting), 13 (American Kestrel), 14 (American Bittern), 27 (tamarack trees), 30 (both), 32 (female), 36 (main), 38 (both), 40 (both), 42 (main), 46 (main, crest), 50 (all), 52 (all), 54, 58 (hawk nest), 64 (main), 66, 72 (main), 76 (both), 78 (both), 80 (both), 82 (both), 86, 88 (both), 90, 92 (side profile), 100 (main), 102 (main), 104 (all), 108, 109 (American Goldfinch in winter), 112 (male winter, female), 118 (both), 120 (main), 124 (female), 128, 130 (female), 134 (injury-feigning display), 136 (both), 142 (main, bottom inset), 148 (Bald Eagle), 154 (both), 156 (main), 158 (both), 164 (both), 168 (female), 172 (main), 174 (both), 176 (main), 178, 180 (main, in flight), 182 (main, aigrettes), 184 (main, fishing), 186 (main) **Gijsbert van Frankenhuyzen/DPA*:** 102 (in flight) **Brian K. Wheeler:** 98 (soaring), 140 (female) **Jim Zipp:** 7 (hawk's tail), 34 (both), 36 (inset), 68 (both), 92 (main), 100 (landing), 140 (wheeling), 138 (main), 162 (main), 166 (main)

*DPA: Dembinsky Photo Associates; CLO: Cornell Laboratory of Ornithology

10 9 8 7 6 5 4 3 2 1

Thundering birds. Booming birds. Drumming birds.
Stomping, whistling and jazzing birds.

NORTHEASTERN BIRDS

Wildlife is waiting for you in the big neighborhood of the Northeastern United States and its forests, grasslands and wetlands. Put on your boots, bring a friend and head out the door. It's time to get WILD About Northeastern Birds!

How to Use Your Book

There are hundreds of bird species that live in the Northeastern US. To introduce you to Northeast birds, this book features 70 fascinating species. You'll find identification tips and information on each species' favorite foods, interesting behaviors, songs and calls, life cycle, migration patterns and more. Most species in the book nest in the Northeast and are fairly common. Some uncommon species have also been included to get to know and support their needs for survival. Consider yourself a "Super Birder" when you have met them firsthand!

The book is organized by habitat—the type of natural environment a bird calls home. It is divided into four sections, one for each of the region's four major habitats: coniferous and mixed forests, deciduous forests, grasslands and edges, and water areas. Within each habitat section, you'll find the birds that live there arranged by size—smallest to largest—according to their length and wingspan.

For a list of the species in this book and the pages on which they appear, turn to the Table of Contents (pages 4–5). The Index (page 199) provides a handy reference guide to the species in alphabetical order. A taxonomic listing (scientific classification) of the birds is on page 198.

About Birds The beginning of this book (page 6) shows the amazing characteristics that make birds unique. It explains how each part of a bird is designed to help it survive. You will also find clues to what is wild, what is a nongame bird and what is a game bird species.

How to Watch Birds This section (page 14) gives you detective skills to find birds while being respectful to wildlife and the outdoor habitats that we share!

When to Watch Birds When are the best times and seasons to spy on different birds? This section, starting on page 16, helps you understand why some birds can be seen at certain times of the day or year.

Where to Watch Birds Turn to page 20 to learn about the major land areas in our region of the US, and tips on where to find birds in each one.

Table of Contents

Appendix

About the Author

Watch for these friends!

Birding Tip

Great ideas for
bird watching success.

Did You Know?

Gee-whiz facts that'll
WOW the whole family.

Do the Math

Brain-teasing bird math.

(Don't tell, but the answers are
on pages 194-195.)

Gross Factor

Disgusting but interesting
facts guaranteed to make
your parents gag.

History Hangout

Cool details from the past
such as where a bird's
name comes from.

Unsolved Mystery

Puzzles and oddities that have left
scientists baffled—maybe you'll
discover the solutions.

About Birds

Chickadees, Herons and Hawks. What Makes Us Birds?

Black-capped Chickadee

Great Blue Heron

Cooper's Hawk

Feathers Birds are the only living creatures that grow feathers. They have six basic kinds. Each one helps the bird with a special job: flight, warmth, information reception, protection, balance, or flotation. The color and pattern of a bird's feathers can also help you identify which species you are watching. Learn more about feathers on page 10.

Ears Yes, birds have ears under their cheek feathers. Some owls and hawks have amazing ears. Feathers arranged in a disk around the bird's face funnel sound to its ears, helping it hear better.

Barred Owl

Lungs with air sacs Birds are equipped with two lungs with special balloon-like air sacs that can spread out into other parts of their bodies. This extra capacity allows a bird to store more air, push air through the lungs better and send more oxygen to its cells. This is important during long migration flights.

Eastern Bluebird

Bones Most birds have strong, flexible skeletons of hollow or semi-hollow bones with many air spaces. This helps them weigh less and—you guessed it—means lighter baggage for flying. For birds that spend a lot of time in the air, this is very important.

Oil Gland To keep its feathers in good condition, a bird spreads oil on its feathers. It gets the oil from the uropygium gland above its rump. The bird rubs oil on its beak, then spreads the oil over its feathers. Cleaning and arranging feathers in this way is called "preening."

Feet Most birds have four toes. Not all, though. Killdeer have just three toes, and all three face forward so the Killdeer can run fast! Toe arrangement can vary. A bird can have three toes in front and one in the back, or two toes in front and two in the back. This arrangement can tell you where the bird lives and how it gets around. You can get more clues about how and where the bird lives by looking at its feet. Are the feet webbed? Do they have large talons (claws)? Some birds have special toes that help them walk upside down, or hang onto a tree while pecking out a hole.

Red-tailed Hawk

Hawk's tail

Downy Woodpecker

Tail How does a bird steer or put on the brakes while flying? By spreading out its tail and adjusting its wing feathers! Each bird species has a tail designed to help it survive. A woodpecker's tail is stiff and pointed. This helps it brace itself against tree trunks while looking for food.

Songs and Calls Birds do not have vocal chords. They have a special voice box called a syrinx. They inflate air sacs to put pressure on the muscles of the syrinx, which makes a range of different sounds. Nearly all birds have some sort of call, but not all birds sing. **Calls** are short and used to signal danger, warn other birds to stay away or announce mealtime. They often sound the same from one species to another. Different bird species can use and understand the same calls. **Songs** are sung mostly by males and used to attract a mate or defend their territory. These songs are complex and are only understood by birds of the same species. Try doing what birds do: sing more than one note at a time, each note at a different intensity and compose 1,000 different phrases! Wow!

Mallard

Bald Eagle

Wings Flying, diving, swooping, hovering, escaping a predator, even landing . . . a bird depends on its wings, which are powered by large, strong muscles anchored to the breastbone. The shape of a bird's wings can tell you a lot about where it lives, what it eats and how it catches its prey. For example, pointed wings indicate a fast flier. Large, broad wings are common among big soaring birds, while birds that maneuver around trees in a forest have short, broad wings.

Crop and Gizzard How does a bird chew food without teeth? For some birds, the food first goes into a sack called a crop, which is located near the esophagus. From there, it is sent into a two-part stomach, where the gizzard grinds it up into smaller pieces. Some birds eat gravel or eggshells (substitute teeth) that stay in their gizzards for grinding hard-to-digest food.

Beak The shape and length of a bird's beak are clues to what and how it eats. How different can beaks be? Spoon, fork, knife, straw, strainer, fish net, tweezers, pliers, nutcracker, saw and chopsticks are a few different styles. Hungry? Select your dinnerware!

American Oystercatcher

Anatomy

It's easier to identify birds and talk about their characteristics if you know the names of their different parts. The following illustrations will help you understand basic bird anatomy. Because these images are composites of many species, they shouldn't be confused with any actual bird.

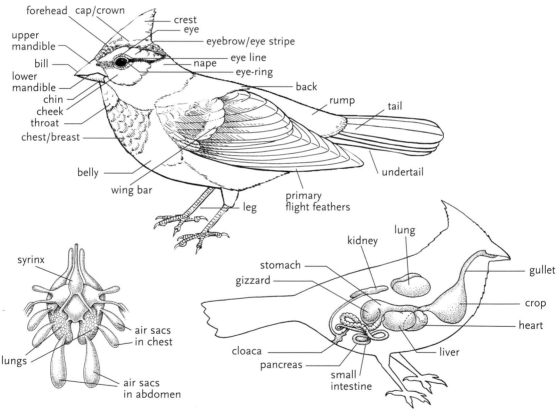

Eggs

Unlike mammal mothers, which give birth to squirming, squalling babies, female birds lay eggs. The shell is made of calcium (the same thing bones are made of) and protects the young bird developing inside it. The shape of the egg makes for a strong shell. It is sturdy enough for parent birds to sit on and incubate (keep warm), yet fragile enough for baby birds to break through at hatching. Some birds lay colorful eggs. The colors can hide the egg from predators or help parents identify imposters.

Almost all parent birds develop a "brood patch" on their chest or belly when incubating their eggs. The feathers either fall off or are plucked out. Blood vessels next to this bare spot help keep the eggs warm. Inside the egg, the yolk is the baby bird's main source of food. The egg white provides water and protein. This food energy, together with a temporary egg tooth, helps the chick free itself from the shell.

Robin eggs

Nests

Bird nests are amazing. Imagine building your house strong enough to survive a storm, large enough for your growing family, insulated—and waterproof. Now, imagine finding all the materials from the natural habitat where you live. Birds do!

Just as there are different kinds of birds, there are different types of nests. Some bird species, including the Killdeer, prefer a simple **ground nest** scraped out of the earth. Birds with such nests may have eggs shaped to spin rather than roll away.

To build a nest that floats on water or balances on a cliff or bridge takes some fancy work. A **platform nest** may be built of small twigs and branches that form a simple base, with a dip in the middle to nestle the eggs.

Cup nests are used by most songbirds. They have a solid base attached to a tree, shrub, or ledge. Sturdy sides are made by weaving grasses, twigs, bark, or leaves tightly together. A soft, inner lining of feathers, fur, or plant material keeps the eggs and young birds cozy.

Keeping a nest safe from predators calls for hanging out at the edge. A **pendulous nest** looks like a sock hanging at the end of a tree branch. It takes nearly a week for Baltimore Orioles to weave together the fibers of their strong watertight nests. They are such good tailors, it even feels like a soft sock!

Cavity nests are used by woodpeckers, chickadees and many other woodland birds. Usually chipped into a tree trunk or branch, cavity nests often have a small entrance hole that leads to an inner room.

Cliffside/riverbank nests are cavity nests that are built into a cliffside or riverbank. For example, the Belted Kingfisher's nest features a long tunnel leading back to the nursery.

| ground nest | platform nest | cup nest | pendulous nest | cavity nest | cliffside/riverbank nest |

Feathers

When dinosaurs roamed the Earth there also lived a prehistoric, crow-sized animal with feathers; scientists believe it was related to reptiles, and have named it **Archaeopteryx** (ar kay op tehr icks) from its fossil remains. *Archaeopteryx* is one of the first known bird species.

Today, birds still have characteristics of their distant relatives. Reptiles have scales of solid keratin. Bird feathers are also formed of keratin, but in strands, which are much lighter. Birds are the only animals on Earth with feathers!

Mallard

Feathers help a bird fly, stay warm and dry, and protect their skin. Feathers allow birds to swim through the water and fly through the air with less friction (which makes these jobs much easier). For some birds, such as owls, feathers quiet the sound of their flight. Feathers can be camouflaged, to help a bird hide from predators, or occur in bright colors to show off during courtship. Whew—feathers do a lot for birds!

What do birds do when their feathers start to get old? They molt (or shed) the old ones and replace them with new feathers one or two times each year. To keep their balance in flight, the feathers are shed a few at a time and in the same place on each side of the body.

Have you noticed the "goose bumps" on the skin of a chicken from the grocery store? The bumps, called papillae, are where feathers grow out of the skin. At the bottom of each of the papillae are ligaments (similar to muscles) that the bird uses to move each feather on its own, an important function when it needs to turn in flight or slow down!

Northern Cardinal

Did You Know? In herons, the middle foot claw has a comb-like serrated (jagged) edge used as a preening tool. This is called a pectate claw or feather comb. Herons use this claw to keep their feathers in top condition.

CONTOUR FEATHERS: *Zipped in Place*

Contour feathers overlap each other to give birds a streamlined body shape (a contour) for less friction, faster flight, and faster diving in the water. Contour feathers are found on the body, wings and tail. Contour feathers have a central shaft (rachis) with vanes on each side. Attached to the vanes are barbs. On each side of the barbs are small barbules that make a "zipper" to hold the feather barbs together. When the barbs unzip, the bird uses its beak to zip them back together while preening.

DOWN FEATHERS: *Keeping Warm*

Down feathers do not "zip" together like contour feathers, but stay fluffy. The air spaces hold the bird's body heat close like a warm blanket. Young birds often have down first, to keep their small bodies warm until their contour and other body feathers grow in. Adult birds' down feathers are located under their contour feathers.

SEMIPLUME FEATHERS: *Support and Warmth*

Semiplume feathers, which are found beneath the contour feathers, are a cross between a contour and a down feather. They have a stiff shaft, but also have soft down vanes that act like extra insulation.

FILOPLUME FEATHERS: *Information Receivers*

Filoplume feathers are tiny, hair-like feathers comprised of a long central shaft tipped with a tuft of barbules. They help a bird adjust the position of its flight feathers. These sensitive feathers move with the slightest breeze, sending information to the nerve cells at their bases. Vibrations from the filoplume feathers tell the bird when to adjust its contour feathers for better flight.

BRISTLE FEATHERS: *Sense, Guard and Guide*

Bristle feathers are stiff, hair-like feathers with a firm central shaft. They are found near the eyes, nostrils and beak, and may help protect the bird's eyes, help it to locate food, and funnel prey (such as flying insects) into its mouth.

POWDER DOWN FEATHERS: *Talcum Powder Protection*

Powder down feathers, found on birds such as Great Blue Herons (page 186) and Great Egrets (page 182), are never shed, but grow all the time. The ends break down into a waxy powder that protects the bird's skin from moisture and damage.

What is Wild?

Is your pet parakeet wild? It may act wild at times, but pets and farm animals are not wild. They are domesticated animals that depend on people for survival. Wild birds find their own food, water, shelter and a place to nest and raise their young.

Wild birds are not owned by people. They are a part of the greater global environment. In the Northeastern US, wildlife biologists and managers study wild birds and their habitats. The information is used to make laws that protect wildlife and wild places. Conservation officers make sure everyone follows these rules, and you can help! Law-breakers can be turned in to the game department of your state or district's resources agency (page 196). People that call remain unidentified. Together, we can make sure Northeastern birds are around for a long time.

Leave Wild Things Wild

Wild birds and animals were once considered unlimited resources. They were killed for their meat, feathers and hides without seasons or limits. By the late 1800s, unregulated market hunting (along with habitat destruction) caused many species—from the American Bison to the Great Egret—to almost disappear forever. The Passenger Pigeon, which once darkened the skies with its huge flocks, eventually became extinct.

Fortunately, laws like the Lacey Act and the Migratory Bird Treaty Act helped protect other wild birds before it was too late. These laws governed the harvest of migratory birds, including their eggs, nests and feathers. Today, many state and federal laws protect wild birds, animals and the habitats they need to survive.

Great Egret

The eggs shown in this book are from a famous collection of eggs gathered by Iowa farmer Ralph Handsaker in the late 1800s and early 1900s. Although wild bird eggs are now protected, in that era collecting eggs was a popular hobby for naturalists. Handsaker's collection consists of nearly 4,000 eggs from 400 species of birds found around the world. It is the focal point of the book *Oology and Ralph's Talking Eggs* by biologist Carrol Henderson. The collection is now at the Peabody Museum of Natural History at Yale University.

It's tempting to enjoy nature by taking it home with us. But it's important to keep wild things wild. Leave eggs, nests and baby birds in their natural habitat.

Game or Nongame Wildlife?

Northern Bobwhite

Wildlife that can be hunted under state law, such as the Northern Bobwhite, is called **game wildlife**. The Department of Natural Resources (DNR) in each northeastern state regulates hunting so it does not threaten game bird populations. For their part, hunters buy licenses and stamps, and pay special taxes on hunting gear; this raises millions of dollars for habitat protection and management that benefits all wildlife.

Birds that cannot be hunted legally are considered **nongame wildlife**. This book is mostly about nongame birds.

Each state or district's resources agency keeps a special eye on hundreds of species of birds, animals, reptiles and amphibians. Donations to state Nongame Fish and Wildlife Funds through a special check-off on state income tax forms help the programs conduct important research, habitat protections and other management efforts. Ask your parents to show their support for your state's endangered, threatened and nongame wildlife by purchasing a wildlife habitat license plate for their vehicle and/or making a donation.

What's in a Name? Binomial Nomenclature

Some people call this bird a kestrel; some a sparrow hawk; and still others call it a killy hawk after its call, "killy, killy, killy." So, which is correct? In the Northeastern US, the official common name of this small falcon is American Kestrel. But a species' common name can be different from place to place; especially if the people speak a different language.

Scientists saw the problem with common names and decided that each living thing needed a name that was exactly the same all over the world. They developed a system of scientific names called **binomial nomenclature** (by-no-me-all no-men-clay-chur).

Whether you're in Maine or Madagascar, a bird's scientific name is always in the same language: **Latin**. Scientific names are written in *italic*, or slanted, letters. Each scientific name has two words. The first is always capitalized and is the genus, meaning the big group it belongs in. The second word is not capitalized and is the species. The American Kestrel's scientific name is *Falco sparverius*. Knowing this, you're well on your way to becoming a citizen scientist.

American Kestrel

How to Watch Birds

We live in a big neighborhood! In the Northeastern US, we share our land with wildlife neighbors that depend on us to treat them with respect and care. Here are some tips for successful wildlife watching and being a responsible next-door neighbor to wildlife.

To Find One, Be One!

Your best chance of spying on wildlife is by thinking like a bird.

American Bittern

MOVE SLOWLY AND BLEND IN

Sudden movements may startle wildlife. Take a lesson from the American Bittern, a bird found around shallow wetlands and lake edges. The bittern eats small prey such as crayfish, frogs and fish. It catches them by S-L-O-W-L-Y stalking along shorelines. The bittern's best moves are almost as slow as the hour hand on a clock. Bitterns also stand still, watching, until dinner swims a little too close . . . gotcha!

Just as moving slowly can help you see more birds, so can blending in. The bittern knows this, too. Its grass-colored feathers are a great disguise. Because part of being a successful wildlife detective is working unnoticed, it's smart to wear drab-colored clothing. Camouflage patterns that match your surroundings work well. Birds will be less likely to see you, and you may get a better look at them!

SHHH . . . BE QUIET, LIKE AN OWL IN FLIGHT

Some birds have very good ears. If you talk and make noise, they will hear you coming long before you see them. Great Horned Owls are super hunters partly because they keep quiet. Special feathers help them silently swoop down on mice and other small animals. When you're spying on birds, think like an owl and barely make a sound! Some birds also use their feet to feel the vibrations of your footsteps. Walk lightly if you want to spy a bird before it flies away.

KEEP YOUR DISTANCE

If you saw a giant watching you, would your legs feel shaky? Wildlife can feel like this if you get too close. Binoculars and spotting scopes can give you a close-up view from far away. If you're not using binoculars, hold your head still and move only your eyes. Animals do this to spy on YOU!

Using binoculars

LISTEN UP!

Bird calls, songs and other sounds can be hard to hear, especially at a distance. To improve your hearing, cup your hands behind your ears. It's amazing what you can hear now!

Wing marks on the snow

If you don't see any birds right away, look for signs they've been in the neighborhood. These include clues such as wood chips scattered around the base of a tree, holes pecked in a soft or decayed tree, droppings, food scraps and empty seed shells, wing marks on the snow, even a stray feather.

FEEDING TIPS

It's fun to feed birds in your backyard. Check the **Today's Special** listing for each species to learn what each bird likes to eat; some include tips on what to put in your backyard feeders.

Snap Photos Safely

Wild birds and animals can be unpredictable. They sometimes move fast, often without you knowing ahead of time. Keep a safe distance away. Many cameras have a zoom lens that allows you to get close-up photos while staying a safe distance away.

You may need to remind the adults with you about this safety tip. If your Mom or Dad thinks it would be cute to have a photo of you standing next to a moose or a Canada Goose, tell them to use the zoom lens and leave you out of the picture.

Souvenir Shopping

Souvenirs help us remember fun times. A photograph, drawing, artwork and your own stories are super souvenirs of time afield. Leave everything else in the outdoor neighborhood—including baby animals that look like they're all alone. Resist the temptation to "rescue" them. Chances are, their parents are nearby.

Look But Don't Touch

Your pet hamster may enjoy being picked up, but wild animals do not. Don't try to pet or touch a wild bird or animal; it may become frightened and bite, peck, or scratch. Keep your distance, especially during nesting season.

If you really want to give wildlife a "hug," build a birdhouse or backyard feeder. Leave our natural habitats the way they were when you found them. Then give yourself a pat on the back for being a responsible wildlife neighbor.

When to Watch Birds

Day, night, summer, winter. **When is the best time to spy on birds?**
Look for the **clues**.

Birds Move When they are the least likely to be seen and caught by a predator; their food is available; they need the most energy and refueling; and when they need to, according to the changing seasons.

DAYTIME = DIURNAL

Birds that are active during the day and sleep at night are called diurnal. Why daytime? Think like the bird. For example, hummingbirds are active during the day because the flowers that hold the nectar they need only open in sunlight.

TWILIGHT = CREPUSCULAR

Many animals are active at dawn (when the sun is just coming up) and at dusk (when the sun is going down). Why dawn and dusk? There is enough light for the animals to see where they need to go, but not enough for some predators to hunt them. At twilight they appear like faint shadows.

NIGHTTIME = NOCTURNAL

Birds that are active at night and sleep during the day are called nocturnal. These animals have special adaptations for being up all night. Owls have excellent hearing and special nighttime and daytime vision.

Journaling and Phenology

Phenology is the study of the seasonal changes and movements of nature. The return of the first robin in spring; the migration of monarch butterflies; the first and last snow of the year; and the first ground squirrel you spy after winter hibernation, are all part of phenology in the Northeastern US. Wildlife biologists and ornithologists use phenology records to help them understand the needs and behaviors of birds.

You can be a part of ongoing wildlife studies by keeping a journal. It's as simple as writing in a notebook or on a calendar. Get started with the journal section beginning on page 188. Journals are fun to look back on. Plus, your addition to the records of the Northeastern US could help scientific research. Be a citizen scientist.

Let's start a journal to record your adventures as an outdoor detective!
SEE HOW MANY BIRDS YOU CAN FIND

YOU MIGHT INCLUDE:
• size, shape, field marks
• type of bill and feet
• shape of wings and tail
• feather color and pattern

Sample Journal Entry

Today I was looking in my binoculars and I saw a female Robin feeding her chicks. They were in my neighbor's tree on 5/13/10. The chicks were small and gray. They had bright yellow beaks. The female was brown with an orange belly, feet and beak. Her nest was made of sticks and twigs. She was very cool.

OTHER NOTES YOU MAY WANT TO INCLUDE:
• Date, time and habitat
• What the bird was doing (behavior)
• Song/call
• Alone, pair or group of birds
• Flight pattern
• Other signs like tracks, scat (droppings), nests, eggs, wood chips, wing marks in snow, ice crystals from a snow burrow

188

Seasons

Understanding how the changing seasons affect Northeastern birds will bring you wildlife watching success.

SPRING

Once the ice leaves the open waters of the Northeast, listen and watch overhead for returning birds. Look for waterfowl, hawks and blackbirds to lead the way. Shorebirds arrive in early spring with quick-winged warblers close behind. Birds are busy in the spring, finding a date and a mate. This is when males defend their territory, sing and do an array of tricks to attract a female or two. It's a very entertaining time of year!

SUMMER

Summer Gross Factor On hot summer days, some birds excrete waste down their legs to help cool themselves through evaporation. Gross, but cool!

In summer, birds are busy breeding (mating), nesting and raising their young. Shhh . . . by mid-July it quiets down. In some species, males leave the nesting area in late July or early August for a quiet place where they molt (shed) their bright breeding feathers and grow in duller colored plumage. They are ready for flight in time for migration.

FALL

By July and August, Canadian birds, including shorebirds, begin to pass through on their migration south. Warblers and songbirds are generally next in the migration line-up. They are joined by some resident birds. Many species begin to group up in large migratory flocks and feed heavily in preparation for migration. During September–October, raptor and water-fowl migration is in high gear along the coastline and mountain ridges.

WINTER

In the Northeastern US, winter means cold. Birds that stick around have slick strategies for dealing with the cold, snow and changes in food supply.

To beat the cold, birds grow an extra layer of feathers for the winter, like putting on a winter coat. Some will also fluff out their feathers to create more air pockets, which trap heat close to their bodies. Others lower their body temperatures at night to reduce the amount of energy (and food) needed to keep warm.

Another strategy is to make a group huddle—there's warmth in numbers! And some birds sit on their legs, or tuck a leg and foot, one at a time, into their warm body feathers.

How do the tiny legs of chickadees keep from freezing in the winter? Instead of having their veins and arteries separated by muscle like we do, theirs are side by side in their legs. The warm blood coming from their heart is right next to the cool blood flowing back to it from their legs. Heat exchanges between them!

Speaking of legs, some birds grow extra feathers around their legs and feet, or extra scales on the outside edge of their feet, for use as snowshoes to stay on top of deep snow!

Because food supplies often run low in winter, some bird species store food in bark cracks, crevices and tree cavities. Others bulk up (gain fat) in the fall in preparation for the extra energy demands of winter, while some bulk up before night and refuel the next day.

Because there is less competition for nest sites and food, some hardy birds may take advantage of the situation and begin nesting in winter.

Migration

FLIGHT PLANS: THE NORTHEAST'S FIVE MIGRATORY PATTERNS

Boreal migrants live in Canada but come south into the Northeastern US when their northern food supply is short.

Permanent residents are birds that stick it out and stay in the Northeastern US all year.

Short-distance migrants go just far enough south to avoid the extreme temperatures of our Northeastern winters and return to breed in the spring. They travel to wintering grounds as far south as Texas and Florida.

Mid-distance migrants breed in (or north of) the Northeastern US and migrate to wintering areas in Mexico and Central America.

Long-distance migrants breed here, but migrate to wintering areas in South America. These migrants travel up to thousands of miles on their way from the Northeastern US to their wintering grounds.

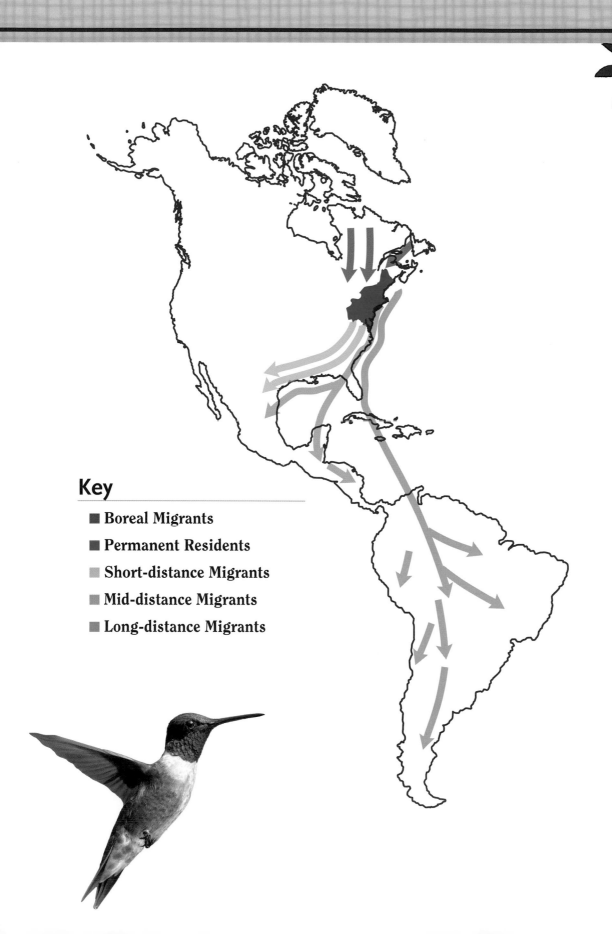

Key

- ■ Boreal Migrants
- ■ Permanent Residents
- ■ Short-distance Migrants
- ■ Mid-distance Migrants
- ■ Long-distance Migrants

Where to Watch Birds

Make bird identification easy on yourself. Narrow down the possibilities by first knowing the habitat. After all, it is of little use looking for a water bird like a Common Loon on a grassland, or a grassland bird like a Northern Bobwhite on a lake!

Northeastern US Habitats

Have you noticed that some wild places look different than others? Some have a few trees and a lot of grass, others are covered with trees, and some are a mixture of trees, shrubs and grass. That is because the Northeastern US has different types of ecological systems, or habitats, and there are many different kinds of trees, shrubs and grasses within these habitats.

FANTASTIC FOUR

The Northeastern US has four main kinds of habitats: coniferous and mixed forests, deciduous forests, grasslands and margins, and wet areas. In each of these habitats, a combination of the climate (weather and seasons), geography, land history and soil support different kinds of wild plants and animals.

Before European settlement, the forest and habitats closely followed the land regions on the pre-settlement vegetation map. Grasslands and water-related areas were found region-wide. Because people have altered the landscape since then, we now have a mixture of habitats across the region.

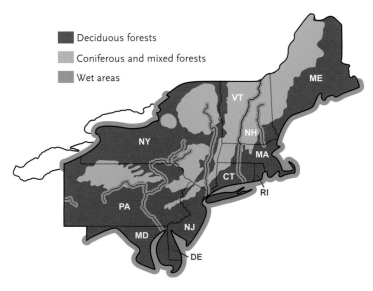

The Northeastern US has four major land regions. The area highlighted in green once supported primarily coniferous trees and mixed forests. Deciduous (red) and water areas (blue) together with the Atlantic coastline were the dominant habitats in the other two regions. Grassland areas are found scattered throughout the region.

To make identifying bird habitats easier, *Wild About Northeastern Birds* is divided into four main sections: Coniferous and Mixed Forests; Deciduous Forest; Grasslands, Edges and Cliffs; and Wetlands, Rivers, Lakes and Shorelines. The 70 birds in this book appear in the habitat section where you are most likely to see them. Of course, many can live in more than one habitat. Some birds are able to live almost anywhere. We have called these species "Super Adaptors." Can you find birds in all four land regions of the Northeastern US?

HIGHS AND LOWS

Most birds are more often found—or easier to see—at different levels in their habitat. For example, you're more likely to see a Wild Turkey strutting across the forest floor than soaring through the air. But just the opposite is true if you're looking for a Cooper's Hawk. To help you know where to look, a large picture at the beginning of each section shows the habitat. Silhouettes of each bird species are placed within it where you're most likely to see them, particularly during the day.

The silhouettes don't always indicate where a bird spends most of its time. Some show where the bird is easiest to see. Northern Bobwhites can be tough to spot when they are on the ground, tucked in grasses and other cover. But they're hard to miss when they fly to escape a predator, or hustle from a feeding area to their evening roost.

Check Off the Coniferous Birds You See!
When you spot birds of the coniferous and coniferous-mixed forests, use these pages to check them off. The locations of these illustrations indicate where you might see them.

☐ Ruby-throated Hummingbird (page 30)
☐ Red-breasted Nuthatch (page 32)
☐ Brown Creeper (page 34)
☐ Boreal Chickadee (page 36)
☐ Purple Finch (page 38)
☐ White-throated Sparrow (page 40)
☐ Yellow-bellied Sapsucker (page 42)
☐ Dark-eyed Junco (page 44)
☐ Blue Jay (page 46)
☐ Gray Jay (page 48)
☐ Ruffed Grouse (page 50)
☐ Pileated Woodpecker (page 52)
☐ Common Raven (page 54)

28   29

Coniferous and Mixed Forests

Coniferous and Mixed Forests

Deciduous Forest

Grassland, Edges and Cliff Habitat

Wetlands, Rivers, Lakes and Shores

21

Sample Page

Common Name
The name used most often in the Northeastern US

Scientific Name
Universally identifiable, two-part name originating in Latin or Greek.

Size
Measurements from the bill tip to the tip of the tail and wingtip to wingtip.

Photo
Most large photos are of a male in breeding plumage.

Field Marks
Identifying characteristics including unique colors, feather patterns, and bill, wing, feet and tail shapes that help you distinguish one species from another.

Birdsong and Other Sounds
Information about calls, songs and other sounds the bird makes—and what they mean.

Downy Woodpecker

Picoides pubescens

Length: 6–7 inches (14–17 cm)
Wingspan: 10–12 inches (25–30 cm)

female

Males have red patch on nape (back of neck)

Females do not have red on nape (back of neck)

White belly

White stripe down the back

Young male has a red spot on top of his head

Black with white spotted wings

"Drum, drum" is rapped on dry limbs.

Black spots on white tail feathers

Built for the Job

The Downy Woodpecker is the smallest woodpecker in the Northeast and the most common. It is buil
to survive and can balance on weed stems and small branches, unlike larger members of the wood
pecker family. Look for this black and white wonder balanced on the stems of goldenrod plants. It i
most likely pecking wasp larvae from inside their cozy gall home. Using its strong bill, long, barbe
tongue (up to four times the length of its bill) and sticky spit, Downy Woodpeckers rake in insects from
cracks and tunnels. Where does it store its long tongue? Curled inside its head like a tape measure!

76

Bird Facts
Interesting natural history information, bird watching manners and tips for success.

Habitat Café
What a bird eats, how much it needs and when the food is available.

Habitat Café
Yumm ... bring an order of crickets, wasps, grasshoppers, ants, beetles, flies, spiders, acorns, berries and fruit. Downy Woodpeckers are omnivorous. Fill your feeders with suet, peanut butter and nuts.

SPRING, SUMMER, FALL, WINTER MENU:
Lots of insect larvae, some seeds

y's Special

ct larvae in
enrod galls

Life Cycle

NEST The female and male make the nesting hole in a tree, fence post or tree stump 3–50 feet above the ground. The hole is 1¼ inches in diameter and 8–12 inches deep. They will use a birdhouse for roosting but not usually for nesting.

EGGS About ½ inch long. Both the male and female incubate the clutch of 4–5 eggs for 11–12 days.

MOM! DAD! Altricial. Mom and Dad put small, soft insects directly into the helpless chicks' open bills.

NESTLING When the young birds are just over a week old, they climb to the top of the nest cavity to be fed. Woodpecker chicks have a heel pad that protects their feet from the rough nest edges. The pad is shed once they leave the nest.

FLEDGLING The young birds can fly and leave the nest at about three weeks of age. They still depend on Mom and Dad for another three weeks.

JUVENILE The young can date, mate and raise young at one year old.

Birding Tip
Make your own suet feeder. Suet is animal fat. In the wild, woodpeckers and chickadees eat the fat from a deer carcass. In town, you can buy beef suet at a grocery store. Place the suet in a mesh orange or onion bag, or pound it into the cracks of tree bark. With the help of an adult, melt suet over LOW heat. Place a string or yarn around the base of a pine cone and dip it into the melted suet. Add millet, peanut hearts and cornmeal. Hang your feeders outside on a tree limb.

When
Downy Woodpeckers are diurnal. They feed during the day and rest at night.

Migration
Permanent resident. Downy Woodpeckers remain in their breeding territory all year.

Nesting
Downy Woodpeckers begin pairing up as early as October or November. Nesting begins in May and early June.

Getting Around
How do they stay on a tree while drilling a hole or searching for insects? Their toes are zygodactyl, which means two toes point forward and two backward. Their long, curved claws are super for getting a tight grip. Their stiff tail feathers act as a brace against the tree trunk. Look for a flash of white while the downy is in flight. The black barred tail has white outer feathers. Flight is undulating (up and down) in a series of wing flaps and then a bound forward.

Where to Look
Open deciduous woods of both old and new growth. Their ability to feed on many different foods allows Downy Woodpeckers to live in many places.

Year-round	Summer
Migration	Winter

Deciduous Forest Habitat   77

When
Times when the bird is active. A bird can be active during the night (nocturnal), during the day (diurnal) or at twilight (crepuscular).

Migration
Does this bird migrate or stick around? If it migrates, look here to see when it arrives in spring, when it leaves in fall and where it spends the winter.

Nesting
When the bird starts nesting and lays its eggs.

Getting Around
Find out if this bird flies, hops, glides, dives, wades, or soars.

Where to Look
A range map and notes offer tips on specific locations to look. Use the extra space below to write down where you spotted each bird.

History Hangout, Birding Tip, Do the Math, Did You Know? and Gross Factor.
Here you'll find interesting facts, math questions, ideas for better bird watching and gross (but fun) bird facts. (The answers to the math questions are provided on pages 194–195.)

Life Cycle
Includes details about the entire lifespan of the bird, including nesting habits, information about the number and size of eggs each species lays, fun facts about what goes on in the nest and how nestlings and fledgling birds survive, the role of parents (or adults of the same species that act as caretakers) in a chick's early life, and the final stages of adolescence a bird goes through before becoming an adult.

Coniferous and Mixed Forest

The seeds of coniferous trees develop inside cones. Most of these trees are evergreen. Their leaves (needles) stay green and do not fall off every year. Why? Turn the pages to explore the coniferous and mixed forests of the Northeast.

Land Before Time

Explore the Northeastern US and find yourself with feet planted on rock from well before even the dinosaurs! Colossal (very big) sheets of ice moved across the northern landscape over the past two million years, grinding down ancient mountains and leaving behind giant rocks and glacial silt from Canada. Huge chunks of ice dropped off and made depressions in the earth's surface that eventually filled with water. The last of these glaciations, the Laurentide Ice Sheet, brought its own remarkable changes to the land 35,000 to 10,000 years ago. The actions of this powerful, mile-high sheet of ice paved the way for the coniferous and mixed forests of the Northeastern United States.

The coniferous forests of the Northeast are located in four separate areas in Maine, New Hampshire, Vermont, New York, Massachusetts, Connecticut and Pennsylvania and include the White Mountains, the Green Mountains, the Catskills and the Adirondacks. The highest altitudes of the Appalachian Mountains provide the conditions for coniferous forests to exist farther south than expected.

Tough Trees

Coniferous forest

Northern glaciated areas have patchy, shallow, acidic soils that are low in nutrients. The weather is extreme. To survive the harsh conditions, coniferous trees are well adapted to the short growing season, cold, heavy snowfall and shallow soils.

Their shallow root systems draw nutrients (minerals) from the topsoil. A wax covering on their needles protects them from the extreme cold and winter winds. The needles remain dark green and do not all fall off each year. This saves energy and provides more time to turn sunlight and water into plant energy (photosynthesis).

Conifers are tough, too: their branches can bend with heavy snowfall. Coniferous trees of the northern forest include red, white and jack pine, balsam fir, white cedar, red, white and black spruce, and tamarack. Some deciduous trees have also adapted to the conditions and form the mixed coniferous-deciduous forests. Deciduous trees of the mixed forests include aspen, birch, beech and maple. Bird species included in this book that inhabit the coniferous-deciduous mixed forests are designated with an asterisk (*).

Wetlands of the Northeast

You can walk on a huge sponge when you venture onto a peat bog. Formed in shallow basins left by glacial ice that later filled with rainwater, these bogs are in a world of their own. The high acidity of the peat (rich organic material of partly decayed plants), cool year-round temperatures, and the limited supply of oxygen due to poor water circulation discourage bacteria and other decomposers from breaking down plant material. Over years, the plant matter builds up into a thick, floating mat of peat.

Tamaracks in autumn yellow

Plants that grow in the acidic, waterlogged peat have adapted to the conditions. Coniferous (cone-bearing) trees of a bog include black spruce, tamarack and northern white cedar. The needles of tamaracks turn bright yellow in autumn before falling off. This trait makes tamaracks a very unusual cone-bearing tree!

Be safe about bog-trotting and venture onto a bog only with someone that knows the area. Visit a bog for a look at Boreal Chickadees, Red-breasted Nuthatches, White-throated Sparrows and Gray Jays. Prepare for a true north woods experience at Acadia National Park, Maine, where many of the birds featured in this section can be found.

Winter Wonderland

You can explore the wilds of the coniferous and coniferous-mixed forests in the winter, too. It's a great time to learn how the hearty birds that live there year-round survive the cold, snow and changes to their food supply. Their adaptations to the cold climate are fantastic! Turn to page 18 to learn more about how northern birds survive winter.

When the snow squeaks underfoot, take a clue from the local wildlife and dress in layers, wear warm boots or snowshoes, take along water and a snack for extra energy and buddy-up with a friend. Be adventurous and, of course, always be safe!

Check Off the Coniferous Birds You See!

When you spot birds of the coniferous and coniferous-mixed forests, use these pages to check them off. The locations of these illustrations indicate where you might see them.

28

Ruby-throated Hummingbird

Archilochus colubris

Length: 3–3½ inches (7–9 cm)
Wingspan: 3–4½ inches (8–11 cm)

female

Females have a white throat
and a white-tipped tail

Iridescent green back
and white-tipped tail

Male has ruby
red throat

Stiff, narrow wings
rotate in their sockets;
large muscles power
a fast figure eight
movement

Light gray-white belly
and breast

Its wings make a bumblebee-like humming sound in flight, and it communicates with quiet twitters and chatters

Smallest Bird in the Northeastern US

Small bird—big appetite. Hummingbirds have the highest energy output per unit of weight of any living warm-blooded animal. What does this mean? For such a tiny bird, it uses a huge amount of energy. How does it supply this energy? It must feed every few minutes and survives the night without food by lowering its body temperature and heart rate. To invite this tiny bird to your backyard, plant tube-like flowers including bee balm (*Monarda*), cardinal flower, verbena and trumpet vine. Include a nectar feeder. You can make nectar by boiling one cup of white sugar with four cups of water for one minute. Change the nectar often to keep your backyard hummingbirds healthy!

Habitat Café

Yumm . . . bring an order of nectar from up to 2,000 flowers per day, with a side order of insects and spiders. Ruby-throated Hummingbirds are omnivorous. Their tongue is longer than their bill, with a forked tip and grooves for the nectar to follow up the tongue.

SPRING, SUMMER, FALL, WINTER MENU:
 Mostly nectar from flowers, with a few insects and spiders

Today's Special
nectar from jewelweed flowers

Life Cycle

NEST The female builds the nearly 2-inch nest cup on a coniferous or deciduous tree twig, usually 15–25 feet above ground. She weaves plant down and bud scales to the limb with spider silk and disguises the outside with moss and lichens.

EGGS About ½ inch long. The female incubates the clutch of 2 eggs for 12–14 days.

MOM! DAD! Altricial. Mom raises the chicks, feeding them a mixture of regurgitated nectar and insects while hovering gently above.

NESTLING Chicks hear their mom's mew call and feel the air from her wingbeats that signal it's time for lunch!

FLEDGLING Young leave the nest when they are about three weeks of age.

JUVENILE The teenagers become adults and are able to date, mate and raise their own young when they are 1–2 years old.

Do the Math

A hummingbird eats an average of 30 percent of its weight in nectar in one day! If you weigh 100 pounds, how many pounds of nectar would you need to eat each day? Do the math and put your answer here. ____ (Check your answer on pages 194-195.) Just before their long migration, hummingbirds double their body mass by feeding on even more nectar and insects. Double your body weight—now how many pounds of nectar would you eat in one day? Do the math again. ____ Wow!

Ruby-throated Hummingbirds are diurnal, active during the day and resting at night.

Migration
Spring Arrival: Apr–May
Fall Departure: Aug–Sep
Mid-distance migrant, wintering in Central America to Costa Rica. Some fly 480 miles on a 20-hour, nonstop flight across the Gulf of Mexico. On their spring return, they take advantage of the sap that leaks from holes drilled by Yellow-bellied Sapsuckers. This is a main addition to the menu until flowers bloom.

Nesting
Begin nesting in May–June in the Northeastern states.

Getting Around
Masters of movement, they fly backward, forward, upside down and hover in one place. They are known to fly 60 miles per hour with up to 75 wingbeats per second! Hummingbirds do not walk or hop—they use their small feet only for perching.

Where to Look
Areas with coniferous, deciduous or mixed forests, backyard flower gardens.

Year-round	Summer
Migration	Winter

Coniferous and Mixed Forest Habitat

Red-breasted Nuthatch

Sitta canadensis

Length: 4–4½ inches (11 cm)
Wingspan: 7–8 inches (18–20 cm)

female

Female wears a gray cap and gray eye-stripe; red color below is pale

Blue-gray above and red-cinnamon below

Juveniles look like pale versions of adults

Male wears a black cap

Black eyes hidden in a black stripe; white eyebrow stripe

White chin

"Yank, yank!"
Both male and female make this call.

Fancy Forest Footwork

Head up, head down, turn around . . . How does a Red-breasted Nuthatch perform this fancy footwork? It has specially designed feet and toes. The first toe (hallux) is pointed to the back and the other three toes are jointed at the base and pointed forward. Like a mountaineer uses a pick when climbing up or down a steep slope, a nuthatch uses its hallux (first toe). While one foot is being moved, the hallux on the other foot is mounted into tree bark like a pick for support. When you see this tree climber upside down and headfirst, be amazed, he/she is an experienced tree-ainer!

Habitat Café

Yumm . . . bring an order of forest insects and seeds. Red-breasted Nuthatches are insectivores and granivores (seed eaters). Fill your bird feeders with seeds and suet for these backyard visitors.

Today's Special

peanut butter topped with sunflower seeds
BIRD FEEDER TREAT

SPRING, SUMMER, FALL MENU:
 Mostly insects, some seeds

WINTER MENU:
 More seeds than summer, but still mostly insects

Life Cycle

NEST Both parents hollow out a hole in a soft branch or stub of a dead tree, 5–40 feet above the ground. They may recycle a woodpecker hole. This deep hole is built up with shredded bark, grass and leaves. Mom lines the nest with feathers, fur and moss and puts a mat of sticky tree sap around the hole to keep out predators.

EGGS Almost ¾ inch long. The female incubates the clutch of 4–7 eggs for 12 days.

MOM! DAD! Altricial. With gummy resin around the nest hole, parents do not enter the nest after the first week. Instead, the young open their beaks close to the entrance hole for food delivery. Chicks poke their little rumps out of the nest for fecal sac (diaper) pick-up.

NESTLING Just before the young leave the nest, Mom and Dad put clumps of mammal fur on the sticky resin of the entrance hole.

FLEDGLING They leave the nest at about three weeks of age.

JUVENILE They search out other teens to form flocks during winter months.

Gross Factor

What is that white stuff on your car window? Bird droppings. Three kinds of wastes leave a bird's body in one package. The dark part is the feces (food waste from the intestine). The white part includes urates and urine, two kinds of waste filtered from the blood by the kidneys. Birds have the ability to conserve water by making their urine concentrated and chalky rather than liquid. Berry- and seed-eaters may have purple or green droppings. Insect- or animal-eaters often have darker brown parts to their droppings. Gross.

When
Diurnal. They feed during the day and rest at night.

Migration
Permanent residents to short-distance migrants moving around the coniferous forests of the Northeast with the changing seasons. In fall, winter and early spring they move to wooded areas with the most food sources, especially cone seed sources. They return to their breeding areas in the spring to nest. In some years, birds from Canada move into the Northeastern US in search of seeds from cones. These irruptions (large temporary increases in numbers) may occur in 2-3 year cycles.

Nesting
Nest mainly in the coniferous forests of the north beginning in April–May.

Getting Around
Zooming through the forests, this bird stops only to pick up a seed or insect. It wedges the seed in a tree bark crack and hacks it open with blows from its sharp bill. Zoooom, it is off again in its fast, short flight to another tree!

Where to Look
Coniferous and mixed coniferous-deciduous forests and backyard winter bird feeders.

Year-round	Summer
Migration	Winter

Coniferous and Mixed Forest Habitat

33

Brown Creeper

Certhia americana

Length: 5–5½ inches (12–14 cm)
Wingspan: 7–8 inches (17–20 cm)

hunting
for
insects

Whitish eyebrow
above dark eye

Short legs keep
the creeper close
against the tree

Three front toes joined
at the base for added
support; long, sharp,
curved claws give
extra grip

Females and males are
brown with buff-white
streaks, just like the tree
bark they creep on; they
are white below with a
rusty colored rump

Stiff, long tail
feathers used
as a brace

"Trees, trees, trees,
see the trees." Males
sing this territory song in
spring and summer until
the young chicks leave the
hidden nest.

The Great Scavenger Hunt

The Brown Creeper scavenger-hunts for insects in the cracks of tree trunks. Finding the prize is a matter of direction—it creeps UP trees headfirst. Starting at the bottom of the trunk, a Brown Creeper climbs up, sometimes spiraling around the tree like a stripe around a candy cane. When it gets close to the top, it flies to the bottom of a nearby tree to begin its hunt again. Another hunter—the nuthatch—goes DOWN trees headfirst to find insects. These different views give both species a good chance of finding insects missed by the other. This makes winners out of both players. Teamwork.

Habitat Café

Yumm . . . bring an order of ants, caterpillars, insect eggs and larvae, moths, beetles and spiders. Brown Creepers are insectivores. Their long, thin, down-curved bill gleans (picks up) insects from tree bark cracks.

 SPRING, SUMMER, FALL MENU:
Mostly insects, some seeds

 WINTER MENU:
More seeds than summer, but still mostly insects

Life Cycle

NEST With spider webs, the female attaches twigs, leaves and shreds of bark to make a hammock-like nest behind a loose piece of bark on the side of a dead or dying tree. The inner nest cup is lined with fine bark shreds and moss to keep the eggs and chicks warm.

EGGS Slightly longer than ½ inch. The female incubates the clutch of 5–6 eggs for 14–15 days.

MOM! DAD! Altricial. Mom broods the chicks for the first 10 days. Both parents feed the chicks and do their part in chick diaper duty from the time the chicks hatch until they are 5–6 weeks of age.

NESTLING The chicks hatch with a very funny feather-style. They have absolutely no feathers except for some gray down arranged in rows just above both their eyes!

FLEDGLING They leave the nest at 1½ weeks of age. At night the young come together in a circle, with heads facing inward and the feathers on their necks and shoulders fluffed out.

JUVENILE At one year old, the birds are mature enough to date, mate, nest and raise their own young.

Did You Know?

Take a trip to one of the Northeast's many nature centers and wild outdoor areas and get to know Brown Creepers firsthand. See pages 196–197 for a list of resources for learning more about the natural areas of the great Northeast. Take along your wildlife watching manners and plan for fun! In the meantime, set out suet and mealworms, and smash peanut butter into tree bark cracks to invite creepers to the wildlife area in your own yard.

When
Diurnal. They feed during the day and rest at night.

Migration
Permanent resident to short-distance migrant, with some overwintering in the Northeast. In September–November, they move to deciduous and wooded areas in towns and forested areas in warmer parts of the region. Others may migrate as far south as the mid- to southern US.

Nesting
Brown Creepers begin nesting in May–June in the Northeastern US.

Getting Around
Parent creepers teach their young to act like a leaf and flatten out when danger is near. They make short flights from tree to tree when feeding. In keeping with their spiral pattern of foraging up a tree, the male and female fly around a tree when they perform their dating and mating dance.

Where to Look
Mature, old growth coniferous and mixed coniferous-deciduous forests, and timbered swamps with dead or dying nesting trees.

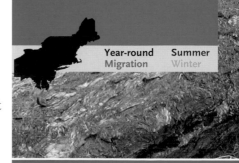

Year-round   Summer
Migration   Winter

Coniferous and Mixed Forest Habitat

Boreal Chickadee

Poecile hudsonica

Length: 5–5½ inches (12–14 cm)
Wingspan: 8 inches (20 cm)

Color varies from grayish brown to brownish gray

Brown cap and back

Females and males look the same

Rusty colored sides

"Pst-zee-zee-zee!" This soft song is sung up to 60 times per hour. When incubation starts, it drops to only 30.

Hide and Seek

Cold, it is very cold in the coniferous forests of northern New England in the winter. The weather changes often. To survive, Boreal Chickadees have become champion adaptors. For these tiny birds, having enough fuel to keep warm is a matter of hide and seek. Chickadees hide seeds and insects in the cracks of tree bark, branches and under needles in late summer and fall and then seek them when the weather is too cold or snowy for hunting. Before nightfall, they can gain 10 percent of their weight in body fat. They use this fatty fuel overnight and rebuild it again the next day. On a winter night, their body temperature drops as much as 20 degrees, using far less fuel to stay warm.

Habitat Café

Yumm . . . bring an order of caterpillars, wasps, bees, ants, beetles, bugs, spiders and tree seeds—hemlock, fir, pine and spruce. Boreal Chickadees are omnivorous. Chickadees use spit, spider web silk, or insect cocoon silk to hold a seed or insect in a hiding place.

Today's Special
peanut butter and suet
BIRD FEEDER TREAT

SPRING, SUMMER, FALL MENU:
🐜 Lots of insects, some seeds

WINTER MENU:
🐜 Equal amounts of insects and seeds

Life Cycle

NEST The nest hole is made by another animal or made new by chickadees in the soft, rotten wood of a tree trunk. The female does most of the work, hammering wood chips loose and tossing or carrying them out. The nest hole is lined with moss and animal fur.

EGGS Almost ¾ inch long. The female incubates the clutch of 6–7 eggs for 12–15 days. She eats the egg shells once the chicks have hatched. Yum, calcium.

MOM! DAD! Altricial. Both parents feed the newly hatched, blind and naked chicks. Delivering over 20 meals per hour can keep a parent bird very busy. For each meal there is a fecal sac (diaper) to carry away.

NESTLING The chicks grow white down and then full feathers.

FLEDGLING At 1½ weeks of age, they leave the nest and soon fly. Parents bring food to the chicks but in time the chicks feed themselves.

JUVENILE The teens leave the area of their parents to join a winter flock away from their parents' territory. They are ready to mate and raise their own young the following spring.

Did You Know?

Do Chickadees remember where they store their snacks? Research shows that during the fall, chickadees can produce new brain cells to handle the additional memory needed to recover the cached food in winter. They likely do not remember where every seed is hidden allowing other wildlife to benefit. In years when there is an outbreak of spruce budworms in the coniferous forest, more Boreal Chickadees are around. Foresters have a message for these worm-eaters: Thank you!

When

Diurnal. They feed during the day and rest at night.

Migration
Permanent resident. During the summer breeding season, they are in pairs, nesting and raising young. The rest of the year they flock together.

Nesting
Nest in the coniferous forests of the north beginning May–June.

Getting Around
Boreal Chickadees hop from branch to branch and on the ground in search of insects. Short flights between trees are straight and quick. Look for the chickadee's tail to point up when it lands, making a "V" with its body. It quickly lowers its tail for balance.

Where to Look
Coniferous and boreal forests, spruce and tamarack bogs of the far northern areas of the Northeastern region.

Year-round **Summer**
Migration Winter

Purple Finch

Carpodacus purpureus

Length: 5–6 inches (12–16 cm)
Wingspan: 9–10 inches (22–26 cm)

Crest can be raised, like a spiked feather-do

Back, head and throat are the color of a raspberry fruit drink

White belly and undertail

female

Females do not have any red; they are gray with streaks of dark brown, a white eyebrow stripe and white belly; young look like the female

Notched tail

"Twitter-twee, twitter-twee!" Warbling song sung by males in late winter to spring to show off to females!

Eating Out of the Palm of Your Hand!

You can have Purple Finches and other birds eating out of your hand! Use materials from around the house and make a buddy bird feeder. Stuff old jeans, a long-sleeved shirt and old gloves with recycled papers. Make a head with a gourd or pumpkin using fruit on toothpicks for the eyes, nose and mouth. Get silly, put peanut butter or suet on top of an old hat. Lean your buddy against a tree or bush. Birds feel comfortable near cover. Fill an old baking pan or low basket with thistle, sunflower and millet seeds. Place it on the buddy's lap. In time, birds will get used to the buddy. You can then sit quietly beside it. Next, put the seeds in your lap and the hat on your head. Birds may snack on you!

Habitat Café

Yumm . . . bring an order of beetles, bugs, caterpillars, spiders, grapes, box elder seeds, buds and blossoms of wild cherry and plum trees, and aspen and willow catkins. Purple Finches are omnivorous.

Today's Special
willow catkins

SPRING, SUMMER, FALL, MENU:
Mostly seeds, buds and blossoms, some insects

WINTER MENU:
Almost all seeds, a few insects

Life Cycle

NEST The female builds the tidy nest cup 5–60 feet above the ground hidden on a coniferous branch or in the fork of a small tree. She weaves grasses, twigs and bark strips into a shallow bowl and lines it with soft, fine grasses and rabbit, snowshoe hare or deer fur.

EGGS About ¾ inch long. The female incubates the clutch of 3–5 eggs for 12–14 days.

MOM! DAD! Altricial. Both Mom and Dad feed the chicks and remove the fecal sacs from the nest—diaper duty.

NESTLING Chicks are fed regurgitated (partly digested and spit back up) seeds. Finches are one of the few songbirds that feed seeds rather than insects to their young.

FLEDGLING The young have their feathers and can fly short distances when they leave the nest at about two weeks.

JUVENILE They are mature enough the following spring to date, mate, nest and raise their own young.

Birding Tip

Do birds need the extra seed from backyard bird feeders? Birds can generally survive without the extra food, but it comes in handy when they are fattening up for fall migration, recovering in the spring or feeding chicks. Long, cold winters can make finding food and water tough for birds that stay all year. Once you start providing food and water, keep it up so you can enjoy the birds. Bring these neighbors close enough to get to know them by name!

When

Diurnal. Active during the day and rests at night.

Migration
Permanent resident. After the summer months when nesting and chick rearing are at their peaks, Purple Finches are on the move. By late September–October they begin to move throughout the region including to areas with backyard bird feeders. This movement peaks again in April–May as they move back to their nesting areas. Some may move farther south during the winter months.

Nesting
Purple Finches nest mainly in the coniferous and mixed forests of the Northeastern US beginning in May–June.

Getting Around
Purple Finches hop and walk when on the ground. They flit from branch to branch in short flights. In long-distance travel they have an up-and-down, bouncing flight as they flap their wings and then fold them.

Where to Look
Coniferous and mixed forests, and backyard bird feeders.

Year-round   Summer
Migration   Winter

Coniferous and Mixed Forest Habitat   39

White-throated Sparrow

Zonotrichia albicollis

Length: 6½–7 inches (16–18 cm)
Wingspan: 8–9 inches (20–23 cm)

tan striped

White line over the eye with a yellow spot between its eye and bill

Black and white or tan with white stripes over top of head

The square white throat patch gives this bird its name

Brown back

Juveniles are more dully colored than adults, and have no throat patch

Gray underside

"Old Sam Pea-body, Pea-body, Pea-body."
Translation:
"This is my space."

Color-coded Birds

Hold tight, these birds are color-coded by the stripes on top of their head. Why? It appears to determine which birds are more aggressive and defend their territory and which ones are homebodies and take care of the young ones. White stripes identify a strong territory defender. Tan stripes identify a homebody. How does this work? Males almost always pair up with an oppositely colored female. This ensures that one is home with the chicks while the other is keeping out intruders. It doesn't make any difference which is the male or female. Females with white head stripes even sing the male territory song. Tan-striped females do not. Get out your binoculars—color-coded birds may be in the area.

Habitat Café

Today's Special
snails

Yumm . . . bring an order caterpillars, ants, beetles, bugs, spiders and snails, and fruit, berries and seeds of plants. White-throated Sparrows are omnivorous.

SPRING, SUMMER, FALL MENU:
Equal amounts of insects and seeds

WINTER MENU:
Lots of seeds, a few insects

Life Cycle

NEST The female builds the bulky nest cup within three feet of the ground. Often, it is hidden in thick ferns, on a low tree branch, or a small bush. She weaves pine needles, grass, twigs, bark and moss together. The nest is lined with fine, soft grass and fur.

EGGS About ¾ inch long. The female incubates the clutch of 4–5 eggs for 11–14 days.

MOM! DAD! Altricial. Both parents feed protein-rich insects to the young. When the chicks turn with their backside to Mom and Dad, the parents take the hint and catch a fresh fecal sac (chick diaper).

NESTLING Parents shade the chicks from the sun and rain by standing over them and spreading their wings.

FLEDGLING The chicks are helpless, unable to walk or hop until they are one week of age. Then they leave the nest. At three weeks, they follow their parents, flying like moths around low branches.

JUVENILE On their spring return, they are mature enough to date, mate, nest and raise more White-throated Sparrows!

Birding Tip

Invite wildlife to your backyard. Provide what animals need: food, water, shelter and a place to nest and raise their young. Plant an American mountain ash tree and a viburnum bush. White-throated Sparrows like to eat seeds and fruit. Scatter cracked corn, sunflower seed, peanut chips and safflower seeds on the ground under a bush or low tree. White-throated Sparrows live in the lower levels of the forest edges. Make your yard a welcome place for wildlife.

When

Diurnal. They are active during the day and rest at night.

Migration
Spring Arrival: Apr–May
Fall Departure: Oct–Nov
Mid-distance migrant. Migrates in small flocks at night to the southern US and northern Mexico. Migrating at night allows for calmer wind, fewer predators and the need for less water since they are out of the sun's heat. Some many overwinter in the Northeastern US.

Nesting
White-throated Sparrows nest in the coniferous forests of the north beginning in May.

Getting Around
White-throated Sparrows hop on the ground and through forest plants scratching the ground for food. They glean (pick up) insects from plants. They use quick wingbeats as they fly around tree branches.

Where to Look
Coniferous forests, bogs and mixed forests of the Northeastern region. Prefers the undergrowth and forest edges.

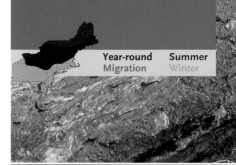

Year-round   Summer
Migration   Winter

Dark-eyed Junco

Junco hyemalis

Length: 5½–6½ inches (14–16 cm)
Wingspan: 7–10 inches (18–25 cm)

female

Bill is pale orange-pink

Males are dark gray with a white belly

Females look like males but are duller with brown back and sides

White outer tail feathers; "Signal of white—a Junco in flight"

"Hack" means "This is my territory." Both males and females give this defense call in all seasons.

Zelda-like Battles

Watch your bird feeders for flocks of 10–20 Dark-eyed Juncos during their fall and spring migration. Pick out the dominant head honcho of the flock. This male sleeks down his head and neck feathers, pushes his neck out and leaps toward other males. The little guys give in or get pecked on the head. Ouch! When two flocks meet, the head honchos may have a battle. The winner is decided in a "head dance." The two males meet face-to-face with legs and heads stretched tall and bills pointed to the sky. *Kew. Kew.* Clawing and using their bills as swords, they have a standoff, spreading their tails like peacocks. Watching this could be better than a game of Zelda. Game on!

Habitat Café

Yumm . . . bring an order of grasshoppers, ants, beetles, caterpillars, spiders and weed seeds. Dark-eyed Juncos are omnivorous. Scatter white proso millet on the ground or snow. Watch for juncos!

Today's Special
black oil sunflower seeds
BIRD FEEDER TREAT

SPRING MENU:
 More insects than seeds

SUMMER, FALL, WINTER MENU:
 Mostly seeds, some insects

Life Cycle

NEST The female builds the nest cup on the ground hidden in thick weeds or up to 8 feet above the ground in a tree or bush. She weaves grass, bark strips, moss and twigs together for the base of the nest cup. It is lined with fine grass, rootlets and mammal fur.

EGGS About ¾ inch long. The female incubates the clutch of 3–5 eggs for 12–13 days. Mom may help the chicks hatch by pulling the eggshell with her bill. She may eat the shell to help replace the calcium her body used to make the eggs. Eggshells also give her the needed calcium to make a second clutch of eggs.

MOM! DAD! Altricial. Both parents hunt for insects, take turns with diaper duty and defend the nest and young against predators.

FLEDGLING Young leave the nest when they are 1½ weeks of age. In another few weeks they can feed themselves and fly as well as an adult.

JUVENILE Youngsters look like adults but with more brown than gray. At one year of age, they are mature enough to date, mate and raise their own young.

Gross Factor

Keeping the nest clean is a chore for some songbird parents. Fortunately, chicks defecate (poop) in tidy bags called fecal sacs. Like disposable diapers, fecal sacs have a strong outside liner to hold the droppings. This liner is made up of edible sugars and proteins. The first few days, parents eat the fecal sacs! Does it make them sick? No. During the first days, the chicks do not produce harmful bacteria; once they do, Mom and Dad drop the diapers away from the nest.

When
Dark-eyed Juncos are diurnal. They feed during the day and rest at night.

Migration
Spring arrival: Mar–Apr
Fall Departure: Sep–Oct
Short-distance migrant. Juncos migrate at night low to the ground. In the fall, some move to areas in the central and southern areas of the Northeast while others fly as far south as the Gulf of Mexico. In general, males winter farther north than females. Some may overwinter in the Northeastern US.

Nesting
Dark-eyed Juncos begin nesting in the forests of the Northeastern US in May. They raise 1–2 broods each year.

Getting Around
Juncos hop forward and sideways on the ground, scratching and foraging for insects and seeds. They fly with steady, quick wing-beats. When flying against the wind, Juncos stay close to the ground. When flying with the wind, they fly higher; this allows the wind to "blow" them along.

Where to Look
Openings in coniferous and mixed woodlands with bushy thickets and winter bird feeders.

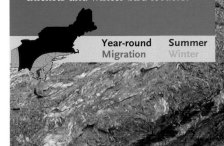

Year-round	Summer
Migration	Winter

Yellow-bellied Sapsucker

Sphyrapicus varius

Length: 7–9 inches (18–22 cm)
Wingspan: 13½–16 inches (34–40 cm)

Red forehead and crown with black border

Female has white chin and throat, may or may not have red forehead markings

Male: Red chin and throat

Black bib on upper breast

Juvenile: similar to adult except brownish on head and breast and faint head markings

Large, white wing patch

Yellowish underparts

"Waa!" This is the call given year-round to signal danger. Drumming mostly by male to signal to female and competing males.

Feathered Engineers

Who has been drilling holes in a nearly perfect circle around the trees? Yellow-bellied Sapsuckers drill neat lines of holes that leak a sweet sap that attracts insects. Sapsuckers then have a two-course meal: insects and sap! Sapsuckers are important members of the ecosystem, called a keystone species. Chipmunks, Red Squirrels and House Wrens are just a few of the many wildlife species that use extra sapsucker nest holes. Golden-crowned Kinglets and Ruby-throated Hummingbirds take advantage of the sap for food when they return in the spring until flower nectar is available.

Today's Special

sap peppered
with ants

Habitat Café

Yumm . . . bring an order of sap and ants with side orders of fresh fruit and tree bast (inner bark and cambium). Yellow-bellied Sapsuckers are omnivorous. They lap up sap with their brush-like tongue.

SPRING & FALL MENU:
 Lots of sap with some fruit and insects

SUMMER MENU:
 Insects with some sap and fruit

WINTER MENU:
Fruit with some sap and insects

Life Cycle

NEST Males arrive in the breeding area a week before females to set up territory. They do most of the nest excavation using their bill as a chisel at a rate of 100–300 strikes per minute. Eggs are laid on the leftover wood chips. The small entrance hole often causes parents to lose feathers going in and out. May reuse the nest hole for up to 6–7 years.

EGGS Nearly 1 inch long. The 4–6 eggs are incubated by both parents for 11 days.

MOM! DAD! Altricial. Both parents bring food to the young. During the first week, they make up to 15 trips per hour—that's one trip every four minutes! As the chicks grow, so does the size of the food prey. Most of the prey consists of soft-bodied insects with any large wings taken off.

NESTLING The loudest chick closest to the nest entrance is fed first. After a few feedings, another chick takes first place in the lunch line-up.

FLEDGLING At about 4 weeks of age, they leave the nest.

JUVENILE Teens stay for one–two months drilling for sap. In fall they leave and join a winter flock away from their parent's territory.

Unsolved Mystery

Please pass the dip. When feeding young, parent sapsuckers gather ants and other insects and may then dip them in sap from a sap well. Does this provide extra nutritional value? Dip into this unsolved mystery!

When

Diurnal. They feed during the day and rest at night.

Migration

Arrival: Apr–May
Departure: Sep–Oct
Short- to mid-distance migrant to southeastern US, and Central America, as far south as Costa Rica. A few may overwinter in the Northeastern US.

Nesting

Yellow-bellied Sapsuckers begin nesting in May in the Northeastern US.

Getting Around

Yellow-bellied Sapsuckers hitch (hop) up and down tree trunks, limbs, or when feeding on the ground. Watch for sapsuckers on aspen, birch, pine, spruce, hickory and maple trees. They have the best tasting sap in the forest.

Where to Look

Northern mixed coniferous-deciduous and deciduous forests. Their favorite trees include aspen/birch, maple, basswood, hickory and maple.

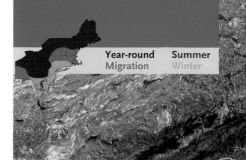

Year-round Migration	Summer Winter

Blue Jay

Cyanocitta cristata

Length: 10–12 inches (25–30 cm)
Wingspan: 13½–17 inches (34–43 cm)

raised crest

Blue crest

Black necklace, headband and eyeliner

Blue above and white below

Male and female look alike

White-tipped tail fanned out means the Blue Jay is about to land

White wing bars

Blue tail with black bars and white tips

"Jaay, jaay!" in the Blue Jay's language means "Danger! Join the mob to chase it away!"

The Great Pretender

"Meow." Is this your pet cat, or is it a Blue Jay pretending to be a cat? Great pretenders, Blue Jays can mimic cats, hawks, screech-owls, American Crows and American Kestrels. This comes in handy. Blue Jays have enemies. They do not like Great Horned Owls hanging around trying to pick them off for lunch. When a Great Horned Owl comes into the area, Blue Jays sound an alarm that mimics a bigger animal, like a hawk. The owl's cover is blown. One jay becomes a very loud and aggressive mob of jays and they chase the intruder out of the area. No more owl on the prowl. Mission accomplished!

Habitat Café

Yumm . . . bring an order of insects, spiders, snails, tree frogs, apples, small fish and the eggs and chicks from nests—along with acorns, seeds and berries. Blue Jays are omnivorous.

SPRING, SUMMER, FALL MENU:
 Lots of plants, some animal matter

WINTER MENU:
 More animal matter than in spring, summer and fall, but still mostly plants

Life Cycle

NEST Both the male and female gather nest materials. The female builds the bulky nest cup 10–20 feet above the ground, hidden most often in a coniferous tree. She weaves bark, twigs, leaves and materials such as string, fabric and paper. The nest is lined with soft rootlets. The male brings her food while she works.

EGGS About 1 inch long. The female incubates the clutch of 4–5 eggs for 16–18 days.

MOM! DAD! Altricial. Dad does most of the feeding. Both parents hunt for food and remove fecal sacs (chick diapers).

NESTLING With eyes closed and no feathers when they hatch, the chicks have a lot of growing to do. By the end of the first week, their eyes are open and feathers are growing in. That is fast growth!

FLEDGLING The young leave the nest when they are about three weeks old and are able to run along the ground with fluttering hops.

JUVENILE Young Blue Jays resemble their parents but are a bit duller, grayer and browner in color. They are mature enough at one year of age to date, mate, nest and raise their own young.

Gross Factor

Do birds have flatulence (pass gas)? Blue Jays do. Adult Blue Jays were observed passing gas by a biologist who was studying them. Now you know even more about bird bodily functions. Word has it that they have a "hiccup" call too. Silly birds.

When
Diurnal. Blue Jays are active during the day and rest at night.

Migration
Permanent resident moving between different elevations in some areas of the Northeast. Watch for groups of jays in September–October and again late April–June on the move looking for a tasty meal. To prepare for winter, a Blue Jay may store several thousand nuts or acorns each fall! This helps new oak trees to sprout, making Blue Jays an important part of the forest cycle.

Nesting
Blue Jays begin to nest in the Northeastern US in April–May.

Getting Around
Watch below the treetops for a Blue Jay to glide on its short, rounded wings with white-tipped tail fanned out—it's getting ready to land. During longer flights to gather acorns, as well as migration, Blue Jays fly above the treetops.

Where to Look
Blue Jays are *Super Adaptors!* They are found all over the Northeast in coniferous and mixed forests, deciduous forests, backyards, forests, parks and even your school outdoor classroom.

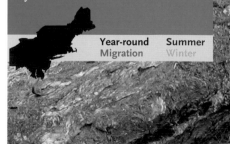

Year-round Migration	Summer Winter

Today's Special
suet topped with peanuts
BIRD FEEDER TREAT

Gray Jay

Perisoreus canadensis

Length: 11–13 inches (28–33 cm)
Wingspan: 18 inches (46 cm)

Short, black bill is used to twist and tug meat from a dead animal

No crest on head

Gray feathers camouflage the jay against the gray bark of a coniferous tree

Pale gray chest

Male and female look alike; juveniles are dark gray

"Koke-ke-keer!" This scolding call can be heard more than a quarter of a mile away.

Hiding the Loot

Have you ever saved your ABC (already been chewed) gum in a favorite spot for later? Then you and the Gray Jay have something in common. Gray Jays have a special throat pouch to carry food in, and an extra-large salivary (spit) gland. They stick their favorite food together with thick and sticky saliva and then glue it to a tree. If they think another jay has discovered their hiding spot, they will move the food to a different place and jam a piece of bark or lichen over it. When the snow blows and hunger hits, a frozen dinner is ready, allowing this robber bird to survive well in the harsh, cold winters of the north.

Habitat Café

Yumm . . . bring an order of butterflies, grasshoppers, beetles, bugs, spiders, ticks, mice, voles, the eggs and young of small birds, blueberries, mushrooms, soft seeds and dead animal meat. Gray Jays are omnivorous. They eat almost any small living thing in the northern forest.

SPRING, SUMMER, FALL, WINTER MENU:
 Any available food item

Today's Special
suet, seeds and fruit
BIRD FEEDER TREAT

Life Cycle

NEST The female builds the bulky nest cup (8 inch diameter) hidden in the branches of a coniferous tree. It is usually 6–12 feet above the ground. Keep a hold of your tissues, they will hijack them and even cotton swabs for ultra-soft nest lining.

EGGS About 1⅛ inch long. The female incubates the clutch of 2–5 eggs for 16–18 days.

MOM! DAD! Altricial. Both parents feed the chicks and take turns removing the fecal sacs—chick diaper duty.

NESTLING Mom and Dad bring spit-covered "baby food" wads in their cheek pouches. Each glob of food is pushed out of their throats into the chick's gaping beak. The dark brown wads contain insects high in protein. Double yum!

FLEDGLING The young leave the nest at three weeks of age.

JUVENILE Teens stay in the area with their parents until June. The strongest bird chases its brothers and sisters away. When spring comes, Mom and Dad chase away this offspring to live on its own.

Did You Know?

When you spy a moose, take a close look for a Gray Jay giving it a free cleaning. Jays eat ticks from the moose's hide. There's a black fly . . . gulp. They catch annoying black flies from an antler perch also. Tasty little morsels.

When

Gray Jays are diurnal. They feed by day and rest at night.

Migration

Permanent resident. They tend to stay in their home territory year-after-year during all four seasons.

Nesting

Gray Jays nest in the coniferous forests of the far north as early as March. An early nesting season gives young Gray Jays time to mature and learn the skills of food caching before the cold winter begins.

Getting Around

Gray Jays are skilled at sneaking up! They perch near prey and scout out the scene (including the baked beans on your picnic plate). Before you know they're even around, they glide on quiet wings, pick up the loot with their bill, and transfer it to their feet for a quick getaway. These antics have earned Gray Jays the nickname "Camp Robber."

Where to Look

Coniferous and boreal forests, spruce and tamarack bogs of the far northern areas of the Northeastern US.

Year-round   Summer
Migration   Winter

Ruffed Grouse

Bonasa umbellus

Length: 16–20 inches (40–50 cm)
Wingspan: 20–25 inches (50–64 cm)

Ruff and comb feathers are fanned out when drumming or threatened

drumming

female

Males are brown, gray, or rust above, with streaks of white

Females look like males but tail bands are not as clear; tail, crest and ruff are shorter

Male has two or more white dots on rump feathers; female has one dot; male's banded brown tail is fanned when drumming

There are up to 50 wingbeats in one 10-second drum . . . drum . . . drum roll.

Let It Snow . . .

How do grouse stay warm in the frigid winters of the Northeast? They pull up a blanket and snuggle in—a blanket of snow. Snow is one of nature's best insulators, with tiny pockets of air that trap the heat of the grouse like a blanket. Watch out for snow-plowing grouse as they fly into soft snow from a tree, making an invisible burrow that is both warm and safe from predators. Getting around on top of snow requires a change in footwear. Each fall, grouse grow scale-like fringes on the sides of their feet that work like snowshoes. The extra width of the scales spreads their weight over a larger surface area, allowing the bird to walk on top of the snow. Put on your snowshoes and explore!

Habitat Café

Today's Special
aspen and poplar tree buds and twigs

Yumm . . . bring an order of aspen and poplar buds, and twigs, leaves and seeds with a side of berries and other fruits during the summer. Ruffed Grouse are herbivores, but they feed only insects to their chicks.

SPRING, SUMMER, FALL MENU:
 Mostly seeds, some tree buds and twigs

WINTER MENU:
Lots of tree buds and twigs, a few seeds

Life Cycle

NEST The female builds a simple nest on the ground at the base of a tree or under a large rock, log, or tree root. The nest is lined with leaves, pine needles and a few grouse feathers.

EGGS About 1½ inches long. The female incubates the clutch of 9–12 eggs for 21–24 days.

MOM! DAD! Precocial. By late May–early June, the chicks are out of their eggs and on the run right away. Mom leads them to areas with insects for the first 12 weeks. She broods the chicks at night and during cold, wet weather until their bodies are able to make enough heat energy of their own.

The chicks add flying to their activities when they are 1½ weeks old. During the first two weeks, chicks eat insects that they catch on their own. By the time they are two months old, they eat mostly tree buds, fruit and seeds.

JUVENILE In late August and early September, they leave the family group and go their own way. Teens look like Mom, but without dark tail bands.

Do the Math

When the air is -27 degrees above the snow surface, it will be +24 degrees seven inches below the surface of the snow. How many degrees difference does the layer of snow cause? Do the math: ____ degrees difference. This is why a winter with little snow is actually unfavorable to grouse survival. Bring on the snow! Answer on pages 194–195.

Answer on pages 194–195.

When
Diurnal. They feed during the day and rest at night.

Migration
Permanent resident. Ruffed Grouse stay in the Northeastern US all year, living out their lives on just a few hundred acres.

Nesting
Beginning in April, listen for the drumming of the male as he sits on a log using his tail as a brace and beats his wings very, very fast. It sounds like a heartbeat that gets louder and faster. He is not beating his chest with his wings; rather, the sounds come from the air compressed by his beating wings. Females are informed he is near and competing males are warned to stay away. Nesting soon follows.

Getting Around
Ruffed Grouse walk on the ground and on the branches of trees and shrubs when foraging and feeding. Their flight is short with a quick burst of speed, followed by a glide to the ground, tree, or shrub. Their short and rounded wings are made for fast takeoffs and turns around trees.

Where to Look
Deciduous and coniferous forests and mixed coniferous-deciduous forests with aspen trees.

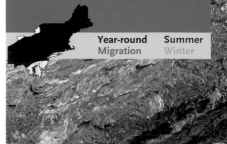

Year-round	Summer
Migration	Winter

Coniferous and Mixed Forest Habitat   51

Pileated Woodpecker

Dryocopus pileatus

Length: 16–19½ inches (40–49 cm)
Wingspan: 26–29 inches (66–75 cm)

feeding young

female

Zebra-striped cheeks; males have a red mustache under their bill

The male raises his red crest to look bigger when defending his area, or to look "cool" for a female

Female has a red crest; she does not have a red mustache or forehead

Strong feet have two toes facing forward and two facing backward for grasping and balancing

"DRUM, DRUM drum, drum."
Male: "This is my territory, males stay away. Females welcome!"

There's No Place Like Home

To a pair of Pileated Woodpeckers, there's no place like their home territory, all 150–200 acres. In the Northeastern US, these old-growth, thick, forested areas are found along rivers and lakes. Pileated Woodpeckers chisel 1–16 holes in a large, soft tree to forage for insects and sometimes for a nesting cavity. Do they use all the holes? Rarely. Extra holes are used by forest mammals, reptiles and amphibians for safe, warm places to sleep and nest. Bird buddies include House Wrens and Downy, Hairy and Red-bellied Woodpeckers. In coniferous forests, Red-breasted Nuthatches and Northern Saw-whet Owls owe a chirp of thanks to the largest woodpecker in the neighborhood.

Habitat Café

Yumm . . . bring an order of carpenter ants and wood-boring beetles and larvae with a side order of wild berries, nuts and suet. Pileated Woodpeckers are omnivorous. They use their very sticky, forked tongue to spear insects. Look for tree holes up to two feet long for a clue that this large woodpecker has been in the area for lunch.

SPRING, SUMMER, FALL, WINTER MENU:
 Lots of insects, some seeds

Today's Special

carpenter ants

Life Cycle

NEST Each year the male and female bore a new nesting hole 15–70 feet above the ground in a soft deciduous or coniferous tree. The entrance hole is 3¼ inches wide by 3½ inches long and 1–2 feet deep.

EGGS About 1¼ inches long. Both the female and male incubate the clutch of 3–4 eggs for 15–18 days. Dad incubates at night and Mom during the day.

MOM! DAD! Altricial. They hatch featherless and with the remains of the yolk sac still attached to their bellies. Parents offer regurgitated insects until the chicks can digest them whole.

NESTLING By two weeks of age, the feathered chicks peek from the entrance hole with a "chrr—chrr" call when they see their parents.

FLEDGLING At three weeks of age, the young leave the nest, flying nearly 100 yards without any warm-up or practice!

JUVENILE For the next several months, the young are fed a few meals by their parents. In the fall, they find their own nesting territory and in the spring raise their own young.

Do the Math

How many drumbeats can a woodpecker drum? If they make 15 drumbeats in one second, how many drumbeats can a woodpecker drum in one minute? Ten minutes? _____ (Put your answer here.) How do woodpeckers drum without getting a big headache? Shock absorbers. Strong neck muscles and an extra-thick skull help cushion the brain.

Answers on pages 194-195.

When

Pileated Woodpeckers are diurnal, active during the day and resting at night.

Migration

Permanent resident. Pileated Woodpeckers remain in their breeding territory all year.

Nesting

The largest woodpecker in the Northeast needs 150–200 acres of mature forest for nesting and breeding territory per pair. They excavate new nesting holes in a tree of at least 16 inches in diameter each spring. Egg laying and incubation begin in May. Listen for courtship drumming—they will even use telephone poles!

Getting Around

Watch for their white wing patches that flash in a slow but high-energy flight of gliding and quick wing-strokes. Pileated Woodpeckers climb up trunks with the use of their strong feet and stiff, supportive tail.

Where to Look

The Northeast's deciduous and mixed coniferous-deciduous old growth forests and areas along rivers, lakes and swamps.

Year-round	Summer
Migration	Winter

Coniferous and Mixed Forest Habitat

53

Common Raven

Corvus corax

Length: 22–27 inches (56–69 cm)
Wingspan: 4 feet (122 cm)

Heavy, black hooked bill

Glossy black feathers

Shaggy throat feathers

Long, rounded wings with separation between flight feathers

Male and female look alike

"Rrock, rrock, rrock!" is given by both males and females declaring their territory.

Black legs

Wedge-shaped tail

Voice Mail, Raven-style

Calling all ravens—food! A raven sends loud voice mail to let other ravens know the location of food. It won't be long before they arrive. The announcement may also be made at the roost where locals and newcomers gather to exchange the neighborhood gossip. Early morning raven patrols along roadways may turn up fresh roadkill for breakfast. Ravens depend on larger predators to kill and open the body of large prey. Cars and trucks become partners in foraging. Ravens rip off pieces of meat with their hooked upper bill and hammer frozen meat with the sharp, pointed lower bill. They cache food in bite-sized pieces, each in a different location. "Rrock, rrock"—you have voice mail!

Habitat Café

Yumm . . . Bring an order of dead meat (carrion), eggs, insects, small mammals, grains, fruit, garbage. Common Ravens are omnivorous.

SPRING, SUMMER, FALL, WINTER MENU:
Animal matter and some grains

Today's Special
grasshoppers

Life Cycle

NEST The female does most of the work carrying sticks and constructing the 1½–5 foot diameter platform nest high (up to 98 feet) in a tree. The inner nest of smaller twigs and plants is made cozy with fur, shredded bark, grasses, sheep's wool and even paper.

EGGS About 2 inches long. The female incubates a clutch of 3–7 eggs for 20–25 days. The male feeds her and stands guard.

MOM! DAD! Altricial. Hatched naked with only a few gray downy feathers, the chicks look like tiny gremlins. The dinner call to the chicks is one short grunting sound from a parent just before it regurgitates into their open throats.

NESTLING Mom makes soft, comforting sounds and gently preens the feathers around the chicks' eyes with her large, thick bill.

FLEDGLING They leave the nest at 4–7 weeks of age when they can fly short distances.

JUVENILE They are mature enough at 2–4 years of age to raise their own young.

Did You Know?

A big black bird is overhead—is it a raven or a crow? Ravens are two times larger than crows and have a wedge-shaped tail. Crows have a square-ended tail. Ravens have a heavier, stronger bill with an angle on the top and shaggy throat feathers and wing "fingers" too. Listen for the difference between the deep, hoarse "rock" of the raven and the clear "caw" of the crow. Raven or crow—now you know!

When

Common Ravens are diurnal. They feed during the day and rest at night.

Migration

Permanent resident in the Northeastern US.

Nesting

Common Ravens begin nesting as early as February and into April in the Northeastern US. Nests may be reused in another year and can become very smelly.

Getting Around

Ravens use deep wingbeats. Look for the long fingers of the outer primary flight feathers. How does a raven dive? It tucks in both wings. Dive and turn? Tucks in only one wing. Watch for halfway rolls, full rolls and in a rare performance, a double-roll.

Juvenile ravens may be seen "playing" tug-of-war, king-of-the-hill, sliding in snow and even hanging upside down!

Where to Look

Coniferous, boreal and mixed forests of the Northeastern US.

Year-round   Summer
Migration   Winter

Coniferous and Mixed Forest Habitat

Deciduous Forest

Birds that live in and around deciduous forests have fascinating adaptations to one of the most diverse habitats in the Northeastern United States: Flight through trees that can outmaneuver a stunt plane . . . wood drilling to challenge the best of carpenters . . . songsters that can out-compose Beethoven . . . disguises that can fool the most clever detectives . . . and some of the most brilliant blues and reds in nature.

On Again, Off Again

The Northeastern United States is part of the Eastern Temperate Forest Biome, which consists mainly of deciduous trees. Deciduous trees lose all of their leaves every year and grow new ones. The species (kinds) of deciduous trees found in a forest depends on the land terrain (hilly, flat, etc.), soil type and climate.

Northern hardwood forests are composed of sugar and red maple, white ash, American beech, northern red oak, black cherry and eastern hemlock. Scout here for Indigo Buntings. At the forest edge, Rose-breasted Grosbeaks chow on tree buds in younger tree stands.

Maple-basswood forest

The oak-hickory woodlands provide nuts that are important year-round food for Blue Jays, Wild Turkeys and woodland mammals that are eaten by Great Horned Owls higher in the food chain.

The trees that grow along streams and valleys (called riparian areas) are fast-growing, shallow-rooted and can withstand flooding. Trees here include: American sycamore, American elm, hackberry, river birch, and the giants of the group close to the water's edge, eastern cottonwoods and silver maple. Eastern Screech Owls search out tree-hole hideouts to perform their magic tricks, American Woodcocks poke the muddy soil for worms and Eastern Phoebes hawk insects on the wing.

The forests along open grasslands and fields host transitional (in-between) shrubs and plants that provide tasty fruits and berries. Watch for male Northern Cardinals flashing bright red from shrub to shrub while Red-tailed Hawks perch on their tree lookouts at forest openings. With the fragmenting of forest tracts into smaller parcels for development, these species have adapted to living in residential and urban areas.

The unique coastal Pine Barrens of Cape Cod, Long Island and New Jersey (among other areas) are home to both common and uncommon species: Downy Woodpeckers, a petite member of the woodpecker family, and stealthy Cooper's Hawks that snatch small songbirds for a quick meal.

Hawk's nest

Colorful Variety

More bird species live in a deciduous forest than in a grassland because there are more habitat levels in a forest. It's easier to learn about these birds if you explore the different forest levels.

Barred owl

The highest level, the top or upper canopy of trees, includes nests of sky-dwellers like Barred Owls. Great Blue Herons and Great Egrets are water birds with long legs, and feet adapted to both wading in shallow water and balancing on tree branches. They build their gangly nests in tops of deciduous trees in colonies called rookeries.

Birds that hunt for insects on tree leaves, branches and trunks, like the White-breasted Nuthatch, use the middle level of the forest. So do birds that favor the seeds, fruit and nuts found there. Some birds nest in tree cavities. Others, like tiny carpenters, build nests in branches—some close to the trunk, others, like the Baltimore Oriole, at the very tips.

Protective Camo, Amazing Antics

The ground level of the deciduous forest is home to birds that eat the seeds, nuts and fruit of woodland plants. Birds like the American Woodcock, Brown Thrasher and Ovenbird prefer the snails, insects and worms found under leaves and in decaying wood. Many of these birds are well camouflaged against the brown and light patterns of the forest floor. Their nests are built in grasses and leaves, under logs and even in structures that look more like a domed oven than a nest.

Male Wild Turkey strutting

Turn the pages to learn more about the birds that make their home in the different levels of the Northeast's deciduous forests. Take this book along on a walk in the woods with a buddy. For a long walk, you'll need an adult. Remember to tell an adult where you are going, who is with you and when you will be back. If your plans change, be certain to tell them right away. Safety first!

Check Off the Deciduous Birds You See!

When you spot deciduous birds, use these pages to check them off. The locations of these illustrations indicate where you might see them.

House Wren

Troglodytes aedon

Length: 4–5 inches (11–13 cm)
Wingspan: 6 inches (15 cm)

Fairly long, slender, down-curved bill for picking up insects

Short wings that are curved in on the underside

Males and females are brown above and light brown below

Narrow tail that is held up, down, or fanned out depending on the signal

"Tsi, tsi, tsi, oodle-oodle-oodle-oodle." When the male's warbling song becomes shorter and quieter, it is a sure sign that the chicks have hatched.

Carpenter of the Forest

The pocket of a scarecrow's overalls, an overturned clay flowerpot, a boot left outside, a mailbox, an abandoned woodpecker hole, a deep crack in a rotten tree—all are used by House Wrens for a house. Watch wrens long enough and you can add to this remarkable list. Building and putting up backyard wren houses is the best invitation you can give to these small birds. Males prepare 2–7 houses for a female to choose from. Before she arrives, he is busy spring cleaning, bringing in furniture (small twigs) and setting out snacks (spider egg cases and larvae). How will you know which house is "Home Sweet Home?" When the female adds grass and feather pillows to her favorite cozy house.

Habitat Café

Today's Special

mealworms

Yumm . . . bring an order of leafhoppers, grasshoppers, crickets, caterpillars, beetles, moths, ants, bugs and spiders. House Wrens are insectivores. The parents will eat snail shells for the grit and feed snail shells to their chicks for the calcium content.

SPRING, SUMMER, FALL, WINTER MENU:

🐜 Almost entirely insects

Life Cycle

NEST The female finishes the nest started by the male and makes an average of 300 trips to the nest in only a few days. She lines the nest with grass, fur, hair and feathers.

EGGS About ¾ inch long. The female lays one egg each day for 6–8 days. Mom begins full-time incubation after the last egg is laid and continues for 12–15 days. The eggs hatch on the same day.

MOM! DAD! Altricial. At first, Dad "beaks" the insects over to Mom and she feeds the chicks. After the first days, they both feed the chicks, remove fecal sacs (diaper duty) and carry the sacs away from the nest.

NESTLING The downy chicks stay in the nest about two weeks.

FLEDGLING After leaving the nest, the chicks are fed insects by their parents for another two weeks.

JUVENILE In summer, wrens leave the shrubby nest site and prepare for migration in the safety of a more thickly forested area. On their spring return, they are mature enough to date, mate and set up house for their own young.

Did You Know

How do bird eggs stay warm? Incubating parents have a brood patch. This bare spot on the bird's belly has many blood vessels close to the skin's surface. During incubation, the blood flow to this area increases, making it a real "hot spot." The parent sits with the eggs directly under the brood patch. Once the parent's job of keeping eggs and chicks warm is finished, feathers regrow and the brood patch disappears.

When

House Wrens are diurnal. They feed during the day and rest at night.

Migration

Spring Arrival: Apr–May
Fall Departure: Sep–Oct
The House Wren is a short- to mid-distance migrant to the southern US and Mexico.

Nesting

In the Northeastern US, House Wrens begin nesting in May. They raise 1–2 broods each year. Watch for wrens in your neighborhood; nest territories are ½–¾ of an acre in size, or an average city block.

Getting Around

House Wrens hop on the ground and fly from bush to bush in search of insects. Their longer flights are straight and steady. If a wren's tail is straight up, the bird feels excited or in danger. Tail down means it is comfortable. A male with a fanned out and lowered tail, head held forward, and fluffed up back feathers, is defending his territory.

Where to Look

Open shrubby woodlands, habitat edges including backyards and parks all over the Northeastern US.
· *Super Adaptor*

Year-round	Summer
Migration	Winter

Deciduous Forest Habitat

63

Indigo Bunting

Passerina cyanea

Length: 4½–5 inches (12–13 cm)
Wingspan: 7½–9 inches (19–22 cm)

Black eyes

The male is deep blue in the breeding season; during the rest of the year, he is brown with a tan underside and a blue rump

female

Females are pale brown with light wing bars

"Indigo" means "blue" but these buntings are actually brown; the blue color is light reflecting off the top layer of the feathers; the true brown-gray feather color can be seen when sunlight is not directly on the feathers

Black legs

"Blue-blue, where-where, here-here, see-it, see-it." The male's spring and summer song. First-year males learn from a male next door.

Night Migration

How do Indigo Buntings know which direction to fly during night migration? Do they use the stars as a map? To find an answer, scientists placed young birds in a planetarium (star theater) and exposed them to the rotation of stars that occur in winter, spring, summer and fall. The birds turned to the north in the "spring" and to the south in the "fall." Were the stars the only clue to finding north and south? Birds also turned north and south based on their hormones (body chemicals). Shifts in hormone levels were triggered by changes in the amount of daylight. Hormone levels may be why some bird species start gaining and storing extra fat and get "restless" a few weeks before migration.

Habitat Café

Yumm . . . bring an order of grasshoppers, caterpillars, beetles, seeds and berries. Indigo Buntings are omnivorous. They glean (pick up) insects from plants.

SPRING, SUMMER, FALL MENU:

 Mainly insects, some seeds and berries

WINTER MENU:

Lots of seeds and buds, a few insects

Life Cycle

NEST The female builds a nest cup in the branches of a shrub just 1–3 feet above the ground. She weaves strips of bark, grass stems and leaves together. Spider webs are woven in and out to hold the grasses and leaves together. The inside is lined with fine grasses, rootlets, animal hair and fur.

EGGS About ¾ inch long. The female incubates the clutch of 3–4 eggs for 11–12 days.

MOM! DAD! Altricial. Mom takes care of the chicks in this family. Dad is nearby calling out warnings to predators to stay far away.

NESTLING While Mom is out of the nest getting food, the young huddle together to stay warm and save energy.

FLEDGLING The young leave the nest when they are just over one week old.

JUVENILE Juvenile buntings flock together and prepare for fall migration. In the first year, young males may be brown or a brown-blue mix with white wing bars. During their first breeding season, male buntings learn the songs of other adult males in their territorial neighborhood.

Unsolved Mystery

Science is about solving mysteries. Using the same scientific method you use to do a science fair project, scientists pose a question and hypothesis, design experiments to test it and study the results (data). Did the results answer the question or provide clues? What is the conclusion? Scientists use the new information to make our world a better place to live. Detective work is waiting for you. Enter your school science fair and solve a mystery!

When

Indigo Buntings are diurnal. They feed during the day and rest at night.

Migration

Spring Arrival: May
Fall Departure: Sep–Oct
Mid- to long-distance migrant by night over the Gulf of Mexico to Central America and the Neotropics. Prior to fall migration, adult male Indigo Buntings molt from their brilliant blue plumage to dull brown.

Nesting

Indigo Buntings begin nesting in May-June in the Northeastern US. Record your nest records in Journal Pages (pp. 188–189).

Getting Around

Indigo Buntings hop from branch to branch and on the ground when searching for insects. Check the bottom of your shoes. Do they have treads that give you better grip when running? Birds need grip, too. Scales on the bottom of their feet allow them to grip tree branches, slippery rocks along lakeshores and more.

Where to Look

Brushy edges and near the borders of woodlands.

Year-round	Summer
Migration	Winter

Deciduous Forest Habitat

Black-capped Chickadee

Poecile atricapillus

Length: 5–6 inches (12–15 cm)
Wingspan: 6–8 inches (16–21 cm)

Short, small, black bill shaped like a cone

Black cap and chin

White breast and belly

Gray back

Females and males look the same

Long tail

"Chickadee-dee, Chickadee-dee-dee" means "Hey, I'm over here!" "Fee-bee, fee-bee" is often a male saying, "This is my space!"

A Tiny Bird With Mighty Adaptations

The deciduous forests of our region are home to a tiny, yet mighty, survivor. The Black-capped Chickadee stays in the Northeastern US all year. They have adapted to the cold, snowy winters by lowering their body temperature at night. This helps them use less energy so they can skip the extra trip for a midnight snack. During the day, chickadees fill up on high-energy foods and stash snacks for later use. A deer hunter watched a group of chickadees each carry away about one pound of deer fat in a single day! They stuffed and pounded it with their small pointed bills into every tree bark hole and crack they could find. A mighty job for a tiny bird.

Habitat Café

Today's Special
spiders

Yumm . . . bring an order of caterpillars and the eggs of gypsy and codling moths. A friend of the Northeastern forest, they eat moths that are destructive to some trees. Black-capped Chickadees are insectivores.

SPRING, SUMMER, FALL MENU:
 Mostly insects, some seeds and berries

WINTER MENU:
 Insects and an equal amount of seeds, berries and fat

Life Cycle

NEST A hole is made in the soft, rotten wood of a tree, 4–10 feet above ground. The female lines the nest with rabbit fur, moss, feathers and even the soft threads of insect cocoons. A chickadee uses a different nest each year, whether it makes its own, uses a man-made nest box, or recycles a cavity made by woodpeckers.

EGGS About ½ inch long. The female incubates the clutch of 6–8 eggs for 12–13 days. The male brings food.

MOM! DAD! Altricial. Both Mom and Dad feed the young and remove the fecal sacs (chick diapers), which are covered in a slippery coating. This makes the job of taking them out of the nest much easier!

NESTLING The young leave the nest when they are just over two weeks old.

FLEDGLING Their pink feet and bill soon turn black and they look just like Mom and Dad.

JUVENILE Juveniles stay with their parents for about a month and then join a small winter flock. At one year of age, they are mature enough to date, mate, nest and raise their own young.

Birding Tip
When you slice a summer melon and carve an October pumpkin, save the seeds for backyard birds. First, spread the seeds on a pan to dry. Then, place the dry seeds on the ground or in a feeder. Birds need water too. Hang a milk jug with a tiny hole in the bottom above a birdbath or pool of water. Birds are attracted to the sound of dripping water.

When
Diurnal. Chickadees feed during the day and rest at night.

Migration
Permanent resident. In winter, chickadees form groups of 6–10 birds, breaking up into pairs in spring. On cold winter nights they may squeeze into their own small tree hollow or share a large tree cavity or roost box with up to 50 birds, including other species.

Nesting
Chickadees begin excavating nest holes in April, with egg laying and incubation during May–June in the Northeastern US.

Getting Around
Look for a flash of lighter color on the tips of their gray wings in flight. When they need to escape a predator they can change directions in just three-hundreths of a second! How do they stay hanging upside down while picking insects off the underside of a tree branch? They have special leg muscles. They creep up and down tree trunks and hop from twig to twig.

Where to Look
Deciduous and mixed forest with open edges all over the Northeastern US.

Year-round	Summer
Migration	Winter

Deciduous Forest Habitat

67

Ovenbird

Seiurus aurocapillus

Length: 4–5½ inches (11–14 cm)
Wingspan: 7½–10 inches (19–26 cm)

orange cap

Rusty orange cap with a black rim

Brown on top

White eye-ring

White below with dark brown streaks

Male and female look alike

Pink legs and feet

"Teacher, teacher, teacher, teacher, teacher, teacher" is Ovenbird for "This is my space!"

Head Over Wing in Love

The Ovenbird has a mating song and dance worth trekking to the forest to watch in May and June. By the light of the sun or moon, the flirting male darts to the top of a tree. From there he dashes through the air in a series of hot-rod zigzags. Shifting speeds, he spreads his wings and coasts gracefully to the forest floor while serenading his gal. Ovenbirds have likely been doing this head-over-wing dance for 10,000 years. Will they be able to continue? Since the mid-1900s there are fewer and fewer Ovenbirds. Roads, houses, offices and farms break large forests into smaller pieces, called forest fragmentation. Ovenbirds need the deep inside of a forest to survive.

Habitat Café

Yumm . . . bring an order of grasshoppers, ants, beetles, bugs and small seeds. Mom eats the eggshells immediately after the chicks hatch! The shells are like a calcium pill to replace the calcium her body used to make the clutch of eggs. Ovenbirds are omnivorous. They eat both plant and animal matter.

SPRING, SUMMER, FALL, WINTER MENU:
 Almost entirely insects, some seeds

Life Cycle

NEST The female builds the domed nest beginning with a small hollow in the forest floor. Using dead leaves, grass, weed stems, rootlets and moss, she weaves a dome, or upside-down bowl, over the top. She includes a side entrance. On the inside she makes a cup nest with fine rootlets, animal hair and fur.

EGGS About ¾ inch long. The female incubates the clutch of 4–5 eggs for 11–14 days.

MOM! DAD! Altricial. Both parents feed insects to the chicks. When young are nearly ready to fledge, parents carry the fecal sacs away from the nest to deter predators.

NESTLING The gray, downy chicks stay in the nest for just over a week and then practice hopping.

FLEDGLING By three weeks of age, their feathers have grown-in enough to begin flight lessons.

JUVENILE At this age, juveniles practice escaping from predators by playing tag. They fatten up on insects before their long migration south.

Birding Tip

How close is too close? You are minding your wild-life manners when your presence does not change an animal's behavior. If an animal does notice you, move slowly and quietly away. Make a wildlife-watching blind in your backyard with things you already have at home, such as old sheets or a tent. Camouflage your hideout and learn about your wild neighbors!

When

Ovenbirds are diurnal, active during the day and resting at night.

Migration

Spring arrival: late Apr–May
Fall departure: Aug–Oct
Long-distance migrants. Ovenbirds migrate at night at heights of 500–1000 feet (the height of a 40–70 story building) on their migration flights to wintering areas in South America. How fast do they fly on these high flights? About 40 mph.

Nesting

Begins nesting in May in the Northeastern US. The nest is so well camouflaged it is nearly invisible! It looks like a Dutch oven, which gives this bird its interesting name.

Getting Around

Ovenbirds walk on the ground and fly low to the ground. Watch for their tail to pump up and down when they fly from tree to tree.

Where to Look

Ovenbirds need areas of deciduous and mixed forests of at least 250 acres in size.

Year-round	Summer
Migration	Winter

Deciduous Forest Habitat

69

Red-eyed Vireo

Vireo olivaceus

Length: 5 inches (12–13 cm)
Wingspan: 9–10 inches (23–25 cm)

Gray crown with black edges

White line above ruby-red eyes

Soft olive-green above, yellowish sides and white underneath

Bill is wide at the base and slightly hooked at the tip

"Ood-l-lee, oodle." Each territory song is only $1/3$ second long with 70 songs per minute!

Signs in the Forest

Imagine walking in a forest with signs hanging from the trees advertising exactly where forest birds can be found. One reads: American Robin is defending his family's nest from this branch. Another says: Ovenbird male is zigzagging here in a wild attempt to thrill a female. Close your eyes and listen to the forest sounds and you will hear the advertisements. The Red-eyed Vireo is a forest bird more easily heard than seen because they hang out high in trees and are easily masked from view. What is not camouflaged is their song: If the vireo's clear, simple song was a color it would be as bright red as their eyes! Males sing continually in the spring, leaving ooo-o-oodles of advertisements for you to find!

Today's Special

caterpillars
mealworms
BIRD FEEDER TREAT

Habitat Café

Yumm . . . bring an order of insects with a side order of small fresh fruit and berries. Red-eyed Vireos are omnivorous, they eat both plant and animal matter. During spring and fall migration they gobble-up more berries and other small fruits than during other seasons.

SPRING, SUMMER, FALL, WINTER MENU:
 Mostly insects and small fruits and berries

Life Cycle

NEST The female builds the open nest cup in the fork of a tree branch 5–10 feet above the ground. She uses spider webs to glue bark strips, grasses, wasp-nest paper, twigs and plant fibers together. She lines the nest with soft grass and camouflages the outside with lichens.

EGGS About ¾ inch long. The clutch of 2–4 eggs is incubated by the female for about 12–14 days.

MOM! DAD! Altricial. Vireo chicks hatch with their eyes sealed closed, without feathers, and with skin so thin that it's see-through. They are completely dependent upon their parents for care.

NESTLING Both parents feed the young. At 7 days old, the chicks flutter their wings when begging for food.

FLEDGLING They leave the nest about 10–12 days after hatching. A few days later they double the length of their flight and can leave the area.

JUVENILE The young are mature enough on their return from wintering grounds the following spring to date, mate and raise their own young.

Did You Know?

Birds' bones are so light that their feathers may weigh more than all of the bones in their skeleton. This includes species that migrate long distances. In 1927, Charles Lindbergh, the first person to fly an airplane nonstop from New York to Paris, France, sat in a wicker chair and took with him only sandwiches, survival gear and two canteens of water to keep the weight low in his canvas-covered airplane. He even tore off the edges of his paper map to reduce weight. Keep it light for a fuel-efficient flight!

When

Diurnal. Red-eyed Vireos are active during the day and rest at night.

Migration

Spring Arrival: Apr–May
Fall Departure: Sep–Oct
Long-distance migrant, flying by night to wintering areas in South America. Some are casualties of hitting tall structures (including cellular phone towers) during their nocturnal migration flights.

Nesting

Red-eyed Vireos begin nest construction in May in the Northeastern US. They may raise 1–3 broods per season.

Getting Around

Red-eyed Vireos hop along tree branches searching for insects under and on leaves. They may also hover for a short time while searching for food.

Where to Look

In the Northeastern US, Red-eyed Vireos are found in deciduous and deciduous-coniferous forests with tall trees including city parks and backyards. They will visit backyard bird feeders stocked with mealworms!

| Year-round | Summer |
| Migration | Winter |

Deciduous Forest Habitat

71

White-breasted Nuthatch

Sitta carolinensis

Length: 5–5½ inches (13–14 cm)
Wingspan: 8–10½ inches (20–27 cm)

female

Females have a blue-gray cap and black on back of neck (nape)

Blue-gray back

Rusty brown undertail

Males have a black cap

Short, very strong black legs for holding onto tree bark and branches

White breast

Long, slightly curved bill tapers to a point

"Yank, yank, yank" means "I'm over here!" Both males and females use this call to check in with each other.

Look out below! I'm coming down headfirst!

The White-breasted Nuthatch has a game plan for finding food. It has to. There are other bird species after the same insects. The White-breasted Nuthatch is a "hop down the tree headfirst insect gleaner." They also work their way up, sideways, while looking for food. Where do they store their groceries? They cache the food in tree bark cracks. Pounding a sunflower seed into a bark crack can open the seed for eating right away, or it can be covered with moss, rotten wood, or snow for munching on later. A male nuthatch tried six different places in the bark and branches of a large maple tree to hide its tasty seed. It was hidden, except from this author (and wildlife detective)!

Habitat Café

Yumm . . . bring an order of grasshoppers, caterpillars, beetles, seeds and berries. White-breasted Nuthatches are omnivorous. Seeds provide fats and carbohydrates needed to refuel during winter months.

SPRING, SUMMER, FALL MENU:
 Equal amounts of insects and seeds

WINTER MENU:
 Mostly seeds and suet, fewer insects than during spring, summer and fall

Life Cycle
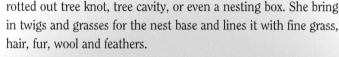

NEST The female builds the nest 5–20 feet above the ground in a rotted out tree knot, tree cavity, or even a nesting box. She brings in twigs and grasses for the nest base and lines it with fine grass, hair, fur, wool and feathers.

 EGGS About ¾ inch long. The female incubates the clutch of 6–9 eggs for 11–12 days. The male enters the nesting hole only to feed the female.

MOM! DAD! Altricial. Mom and Dad make many trips for insects to feed their hungry brood. How many? Up to 22 trips per hour.

NESTLING The chicks stay in the nest for about one month. Parents keep squirrels out by sweeping the nest with an insect (a beetle) that leaks sticky, oily fluid from its crushed legs! They may also sway back and forth with wings spread to surprise a squirrel into hightailing it down the tree.

FLEDGLING The young birds stay with Mom and Dad for another few weeks after they leave the nest.

JUVENILE Juveniles leave their parents' territory to find their own space.

Birding Tip

Mealworms for dinner! Birds that stay in the Northeastern US during the winter need protein to keep up their heat-making energy. Take a trip to your local bird, pet, or fishing bait shop and stock up on mealworms. Simply keep them in the refrigerator, but clue your parents in or worms may make a surprise pizza topping. Place the worms in a flat bird feeder and watch for nuthatches, chickadees, cardinals, juncos and woodpeckers to chow down. Tasty!

When
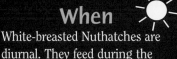
White-breasted Nuthatches are diurnal. They feed during the day and rest at night.

Migration
Permanent resident. They stay all year and use their energy to find insects in the less crowded winter forest. Bird species that migrate use their energy to make the long round-trip.

Nesting
Begin nesting in April–May in the Northeastern US. Prefer nest sites near edges of woodlands.

Getting Around
Nuthatches use their long, somewhat pointed wings for quick darting flights from tree to tree. Because they have a short tail, they spread their feet far apart and at a slight angle from the tree bark for support while feeding. Watch them pick up a seed, fly off to a tree trunk, then hide the tidbit for a later snack.

Where to Look
Deciduous forests throughout the Northeast. Backyard trees, bird feeders, parks, orchards and farm lots with mature trees.

Year-round	Summer
Migration	Winter

Deciduous Forest Habitat

Eastern Phoebe

Sayornis phoebe

Length: 5½–7 inches (14–17 cm)
Wingspan: 10–11 inches (26–28 cm)

Dark head, white throat

Bill has "whiskers," bristle feathers that aid in funneling insects to their mouth

Male and female look alike

White underneath

Flicks tail downward repeatedly

"Fee-bee." This song is used by males to attract a female. They do not need to learn it from another male. Phoebes also make a "chip" call.

Silver Circle of Thread

Eastern Phoebes generally return to the same nesting site from one year to the next. How do we know? Research. The first US study was carried out by naturalist and painter John James Audubon. In 1804, he tied a silver circle of thread to the legs of nestling phoebes near Philadelphia and then recorded the data on the two birds that returned to the area the next year. Today biologists use banding and transmitters for collecting data on the movements of birds. Endangered and threatened species like the Piping Plover are banded and followed very closely. You can observe bird banding at programs sponsored by a local Audubon Club, or a resources agency or Ornithologists' Union (page 196). Fascinating!

Habitat Café

Yumm . . . bring an order of flying insects with a side order of small fresh fruit and berries. Eastern Phoebes are omnivorous, they eat both plant and animal matter. They capture flying insects by hawking.

SUMMER MENU:

 Mostly insects

SPRING, FALL & WINTER MENU:

 Mostly insects and some small fruits and seeds

Life Cycle

NEST The female builds the open nest cup on a rock ledge, bridge, culvert, or the eave of a building. She takes a beakful of moss or leaves, dips the wad into mud and then takes it back to make a circular or semi-circular base. The nest is lined with fine grass, hair, or fur.

EGGS About ¾ inch long. The clutch of 3–6 eggs is incubated by the female for about 14–16 days.

MOM! DAD! Altricial. The chicks break open the wider end of the egg with their egg tooth, making a "T". Their featherless skin is deep pink.

NESTLING Both parents feed the young. In a nest of four chicks, parents may make over 200 feeding trips on the first day alone and nearly 9,000 nest visits in 17 days! The dinner menu is mostly flies and spiders. Scrumptious.

FLEDGLING They are fully feathered and leave the nest at about 16–18 days after hatching.

JUVENILE The young are mature enough on their return from wintering grounds the following spring to nest and raise their own young.

Birding Tip

Nongame and game birds are tagged with bands to aid in learning more about their life histories. The information is used to provide for the birds' long-term needs. Bands provided by the Bird Banding Laboratory are inscribed CALL 1-800-327-BAND followed by a unique 8 or 9 digit number. If you locate a deceased banded bird or can read the band number on a large live bird with the aid of binoculars, report the number, bird location, etc., via the phone number.

When

Diurnal. Eastern Phoebes are active during the day and rest at night.

Migration

Spring Arrival: Mar
Fall Departure: Sep–Oct
Short-distance migrant that flies to wintering areas just south of the frost line and areas with an average minimum winter temperature of 25 degrees F (-4 C).

Nesting

Eastern Phoebes begin nest construction as early as March in the Northeastern US allowing them time to raise two broods over the summer.

Getting Around

Flight is level and direct. Their flight pattern to and from the nest includes a swoop up or down. Phoebes spend very little time on the ground, but when they do, they hop.

Where to Look

In the Northeastern US, Eastern Phoebes are found in deciduous forests and edges close to water, often near rock outcrops, bridges, culverts and buildings.

Year-round	Summer
Migration	Winter

Downy Woodpecker

Picoides pubescens

Length: 5½–7 inches (14–17 cm)
Wingspan: 10–12 inches (25–30 cm)

Males have red patch on nape (back of neck)

White belly

female

Females do not have red on nape (back of neck)

Young male has a red spot on top of his head

White stripe down the back

Black with white spotted wings

"Drum, drum" is rapped on dry limbs.

Black spots on white tail feathers

Built for the Job

The Downy Woodpecker is the smallest woodpecker in the Northeast and the most common. It is built to survive and can balance on weed stems and small branches, unlike larger members of the woodpecker family. Look for this black and white wonder balanced on the stems of goldenrod plants. It is most likely pecking wasp larvae from inside their cozy gall home. Using its strong bill, long, barbed tongue (up to four times the length of its bill) and sticky spit, Downy Woodpeckers rake in insects from cracks and tunnels. Where does it store its long tongue? Curled inside its head like a tape measure!

Today's Special
Insect larvae in goldenrod galls

Habitat Café

Yumm . . . bring an order of crickets, wasps, grasshoppers, ants, beetles, flies, spiders, acorns, berries and fruit. Downy Woodpeckers are omnivorous. Fill your feeders with suet, peanut butter and nuts.

SPRING, SUMMER, FALL, WINTER MENU:
Lots of insect larvae, some seeds

Life Cycle

NEST The female and male make the nesting hole in a tree, fence post or tree stump 3–50 feet above the ground. The hole is 1¼ inches in diameter and 8–12 inches deep. They will use a birdhouse for roosting but not usually for nesting.

EGGS About ¾ inch long. Both the male and female incubate the clutch of 4–5 eggs for 11–12 days.

MOM! DAD! Altricial. Mom and Dad put small, soft insects directly into the helpless chicks' open bills.

NESTLING When the young birds are just over a week old, they climb to the top of the nest cavity to be fed. Woodpecker chicks have a heel pad that protects their feet from the rough nest edges. The pad is shed once they leave the nest.

FLEDGLING The young birds can fly and leave the nest at about three weeks of age. They still depend on Mom and Dad for another three weeks.

JUVENILE The young can date, mate and raise young at one year old.

Birding Tip

Make your own suet feeder. Suet is animal fat. In the wild, woodpeckers and chickadees eat the fat from a deer carcass. In town, you can buy beef suet at a grocery store. Place the suet in a mesh orange or onion bag, or pound it into the cracks of tree bark. With the help of an adult, melt suet over LOW heat. Place a string or yarn around the base of a pine cone and dip it into the melted suet. Add millet, peanut hearts and cornmeal. Hang your feeder outside on a tree limb.

When

Downy Woodpeckers are diurnal. They feed during the day and rest at night.

Migration
Permanent resident. Downy Woodpeckers remain in their breeding territory all year.

Nesting
Downy Woodpeckers begin pairing up as early as October or November. Nesting begins in May and early June.

Getting Around
How do they stay on a tree while drilling a hole or searching for insects? Their toes are zygodactyl, which means two toes point forward and two backward. Their long, curved claws are super for getting a tight grip. Their stiff tail feathers act as a brace against the tree trunk. Look for a flash of white while the downy is in flight. The black barred tail has white outer feathers. Flight is undulating (up and down) in a series of wing flaps and then a bound forward.

Where to Look
Open deciduous woods of both old and new growth. Their ability to feed on many different foods allows Downy Woodpeckers to live in many places.

Year-round	Summer
Migration	Winter

Deciduous Forest Habitat

77

Baltimore Oriole

Icterus galbula

Length: 6½–7½ inches (17–19 cm)
Wingspan: 9–12 inches (23–30 cm)

female

Males are black with an orange breast, underside and wing shoulder

Females are brown-olive on back and faded yellow underneath; wings have a white wing bar

One white wing bar

Young look like female

Orange-and-black tail

The whistling song of adults is as clear, rich and bright as the color orange!

Backyard Buffet

If you live in an area with large cottonwood, birch, maple, aspen, boxelder, or birch trees then you have a fair chance of hearing and seeing Baltimore Orioles. Increase your chances by setting out grape jelly, fresh or frozen peas, apple slices and orange halves. Add variety to your backyard buffet with protein-packed mealworms and walnuts. Baltimore Orioles also feed on nectar. Fill your nectar feeder, and plant hollyhocks, hostas, delphiniums and foxglove. Next, plant their favorite fruit sources like cherries, elderberries, blackberries and mulberries. Finally, lure orioles in with a selection of nesting materials: yarn, string, milkweed silk and dog hair. Sit back and enjoy the show!

Habitat Café

Yumm . . . bring an order of caterpillars, grasshoppers, ants, beetles, spiders, blackberries, cherries, apples and raspberries. Fill a nectar feeder and watch orioles in your backyard. Baltimore Orioles are omnivorous. Many birds can see UV light and many ripe fruits reflect UV light but the leaves around them do not. This allows birds to zero in on their next snack!

SPRING, SUMMER, FALL, WINTER MENU:
 Mostly insects, some fruit

Life Cycle

NEST The female builds a pouch-like nest on the tip of a large tree branch. She hangs loops of plant fibers and long grass around the branch. Milkweed silk is woven through the loops to make a hanging basket 5–8 inches long. The pouch is lined with feathers and animal fur. Set out brightly colored string, yarn, or fabric strips in your yard and she may weave them into her hanging work of art!

EGGS About 1 inch long. The female incubates the clutch of 4–5 eggs for 12–14 days.

MOM! DAD! Altricial. Mom and Dad make about 13 trips per hour to feed their hungry chicks.

NESTLING The chicks stay in the nest for about two weeks. "Tee-dee-dee" means "Bring food, more food!"

FLEDGLING When the young leave the nest, they can fly short distances. Mom and Dad bring the young birds food for two more weeks. They may take the kids to a nearby grape jelly feeder and stuff their beaks full of sticky jelly. Fresh green peas are popular, too.

JUVENILE In late summer, small flocks of juveniles group together and prepare for migration. It takes males two years to look like Dad.

Did You Know?

In their Costa Rica wintering grounds, orioles feed on the fruit and insects found in both the tropical lowland forests and on coffee plantations. Planting Inga trees between the rows shades the coffee trees and makes more habitat for wildlife. Migratory birds depend on habitat around the world for their survival. Well done, Costa Rica!

When

Baltimore Orioles are diurnal. They feed during the day and rest at night.

Migration

Spring Arrival: Apr–May
Fall Departure: Aug–Sep
Mid- to long-distance migrant to Central and South America.

Nesting

Baltimore Orioles begin nesting in May in the Northeastern US.

Getting Around

Baltimore Orioles are strong fliers with powerful wing strokes. They hop from branch to branch to glean (pick up) insects. They can even hang upside down to eat fruit and weave their nests! This is a handy trick to know because it can take the female Baltimore Oriole nearly a week to finish weaving the sock-like nest. That's a long time to hang upside down!

Where to Look

Deciduous forest. Open woods and forest edges, parks, orchards and city neighborhoods.

Year-round	Summer
Migration	Winter

Deciduous Forest Habitat

Northern Cardinal

Length: 8–9 inches (21–13 cm)
Wingspan: 10–12 inches (25–31 cm)

Red crest

Males are bright red

female

Females are gray-tan with pale red on crest and wings

Red, conical bill is shaped for cracking open hard seeds

Young look like female, but with dark crest and bill

"Chip, chip."
Male: "This is my territory."
"Took, took."
Female: "All clear. You can bring the food to the nest now."

Razzle-dazzle Red

Over 100 years ago people often caged Northern Cardinals. The very beauty they sought to capture was lost as the male cardinals' brilliant red color faded. (Today, the Migratory Bird Treaty Act of 1918 protects cardinals from captivity.) The loss of feather color may have been a change from the bird's natural diet. Red and yellow feather color comes from cartenoid pigments. Cartenoids only develop after ingestion of certain plants and seeds, which the caged birds weren't likely fed. Also, male cardinals molt once per year, in the fall. Their new feathers are tipped with gray barbules. The gray feather edges wear down over the winter so that by spring courtship season males are razzle-dazzle red!

Habitat Café

Yumm . . . bring an order of grasshoppers, cicadas, beetles, butterflies, moths, seeds and fruit. Cardinals are omnivorous. When the trees leaf out, they feed on leaf buds and insect larvae. In the fall, they eat seeds and fruit. Young chicks eat protein-rich insects.

SPRING, SUMMER, FALL MENU:

 Insects are the main course, with hearty helpings of seeds and fruits

WINTER MENU:

 Mainly seeds and fruits, some insects

Life Cycle

NEST The female builds the bowl-shaped nest in a thick tangle of shrubs or in a small tree within 10 feet of the ground. Using her bill, the female chews the twigs to make them easier to bend around her body. Then, sitting in the center of the nest and turning around, she pushes out with her feet against the twigs, grapevine bark, leaves, or weed stems to form a cup. The nest is lined with fine grass.

EGGS About 1 inch long. The female incubates the clutch of 2–5 eggs for 11–13 days. The male brings her food.

MOM! DAD! Altricial. Mom and Dad both care for the chicks.

NESTLING The gray, downy chicks stay in the nest for 8–10 days while their feathers grow in.

FLEDGLING When young cardinals leave the nest at almost two weeks of age, they have small crests on their heads and can fly short distances. They perch on a nearby branch while Mom and Dad deliver food.

JUVENILE At one year of age most young have settled within five miles of where they were raised to sing their adult song, date, mate and raise their own young.

Unsolved Mystery

Why do some songbirds rub or hold ants on their feathers and skin? Why does a bird lay on an anthill and allow ants to crawl into its feathers? Biologists have not solved the mystery of this behavior, called anting. Ideas include: ants have an acid that protects birds against parasites, fungus and bacteria that could harm their feathers; it soothes their skin during feather molting; they store ants for eating later; and/or the ants' acid works to ready food for eating. Get antsy and solve the mystery!

When

Northern Cardinals are diurnal. They feed during the day and rest at night.

Migration

Permanent residents. Birds lose body heat through the unfeathered fleshy areas around their beak and eyes. To stay warm during the cold winters of the Northeastern US, a cardinal fluffs out its feathers to trap body heat and tucks its bill inside its wing.

Nesting

Northern Cardinals begin nesting as early as April in the Northeastern US.

Getting Around

Northern Cardinals hop on the ground and take short flights from branch to branch when looking for insects and buds to eat. They clean and sharpen their bill by rubbing the edges on something hard. On winter afternoons, they often become active before sunset, looking for a snack before they go to sleep.

Where to Look

Look for cardinals in thick, shrubby areas of deciduous forests, farm windbreaks, urban woodlots and backyards.

Year-round	Summer
Migration	Winter

Deciduous Forest Habitat

Rose-breasted Grosbeak

Pheucticus ludovicianus

Length: 7–8 inches (18–21 cm)
Wingspan: 11½–13 inches (29–33 cm)

Large, white seed-eating bill

Black mask

female

Female with dark and light streaks on back and chest; White underside; brown tail

Pink-red triangle on breast

While females look the same all year, males change to brown and white during the nonbreeding season

White underparts with faint streaks under wings

"See!" Both males and females sing a song a bit like a robin, but sweeter.

Global Warming and Birds

Rose-breasted Grosbeaks, like other migratory birds, depend on habitat around the globe for survival. How does global warming affect birds? Is spring migration becoming earlier and fall migration later? Are nesting ranges moving north? Birds belong to a complex food web. Birds that nest in North America take advantage of the summer increase in insects (protein) to fuel their chicks' fast growth. This timing has evolved over thousands of years into a synchronized pattern of events. How does global warming affect the food web? Be a part of science and help find the answers. Join the National Audubon Society's "Great Backyard Bird Count" to record events in the natural world.

Habitat Café

Yumm . . . bring an order of tree buds, flowers, insects and fruit. Rose-breasted Grosbeaks are omnivorous, eating both plant and animal matter. They also help farmers by eating crop pests.

SPRING, SUMMER MENU:
 Tree buds, insects and fruit

FALL MENU:
 Fruit

WINTER MENU:
 Insects and fruit

Life Cycle

NEST The loose cup nest is built by both the female and male in the fork of a deciduous tree, commonly 7–12 feet above the ground. The loose and flimsy nest of twigs is lined with fine rootlets, grass, feathers, or leaves.

 EGGS About 1 inch long. Both parents incubate the clutch of 3–5 eggs for 11–14 days.

MOM! DAD! Altricial. Mom and Dad both feed the chicks, brood them and do their part in diaper duty. Parents make 50 or more feeding visits to the famished young per hour; now that's fast food.

NESTLING When danger is near, the nearly week old chicks do their "freeze" act to outsmart predators.

FLEDGLING With such fast growth, chicks leave the nest at 9–12 days of age. The egg tooth used to break out of the shell drops off in the second week. At this stage it would only add extra weight when trying to fly.

JUVENILE In one year, they are mature enough to nest and raise their own young.

Did You Know?

On a moonlit September or April night when you lay quietly in your room, open the windows wide, pull your pillow to the windowsill and listen. The sky is alive. You may even hear the faint migration calls of some of the hundreds and thousands of birds passing overhead along the great migration skyway. Each species has a call they use during migration to communicate. It's a wonder that anyone can think of sleep on a night with wildlife on the move in the starry sky—the stuff of dreams!

When

Rose-breasted Grosbeaks are diurnal. They feed during the day and rest at night.

Migration
Spring Arrival: Apr–May
Fall Departure: late Aug–Oct
Mid- to long-distance migrant to Central and South America. Migratory flight by night alone or in groups of 50 or more grosbeaks.

Nesting
Rose-breasted Grosbeaks begin nesting in May in the Northeastern US.

Getting Around
Watch for the male's black-and-white wing marks during their strong up and down flight (fast then slow wing bursts). When on the ground or along a branch, they hop rather than walk.

Where to Look
Deciduous and mixed forests, edges, thickets, orchards, parks and gardens. For updates on where birds are being seen in your area, information on birding field trips, festivals and more, check out the resources on pages 196-197.

Year-round	Summer
Migration	Winter

Deciduous Forest Habitat

Gray Catbird

Dumetella carolinensis

Length: 8–9 inches (21–24 cm)
Wingspan: 9–12 inches (22–30 cm)

Black crown
and forehead

Dark gray above and
lighter gray below

Straight bill with
long bristle feath-
ers at the base
to help in insect
foraging

Long black tail
with rust color
underneath

Female and male
look similar

"Mew." This cat-like call is given by both the male and female to send predators packing.

Mew, mew

A friend asked me to help find a cat stuck in a thicket. In his words, "The poor thing must have been after all the birds in there." Perched in the berry thicket was a Gray Catbird singing his song collection, which includes calls of a tree frog, a cat, lawn equipment and 44 other species of birds. Gray Catbirds produce song from both the left and right chamber of their syrinx. Both sides have the same range but generally the left syrinx produces lower frequency notes, like a pianist who divides the playing between the right and left hands. Invite catbirds to your yard with plantings of plum, Amur maple, honeysuckle and chokecherry. Add blackberry and raspberry plants and you can picnic too!

Today's Special
wild plums and chokecherries

Habitat Café

Yumm . . . bring an order of fruit from wild shrubs, vines and berry canes with a side order of insects and seeds. Gray Catbirds are omnivorous, they eat both plant and animal matter. They visit backyard bird feeders stocked with grape jelly, sliced apples, peanuts, raisins, broken walnuts and mealworms. Place feeders near shrubby thickets or create a brush pile nearby.

SPRING, SUMMER, FALL, WINTER MENU:
Mostly fruit with some insects, seeds and nuts

Life Cycle

NEST The female builds the deep cup nest in a vine, shrub or low tree 3–10 feet above the ground. She gathers grape or cedar bark, twigs, grass and stems. She then weaves a nest basket and lines it with fine rootlets.

EGGS About 1 inch long. The clutch of 3–5 eggs is incubated by the female for about 12–13 days. Dad guards the nest.

MOM! DAD! Altricial. Mom and Dad feed the nestlings protein-packed insects to fuel their early growth spurt.

NESTLING Direct sun can be hot on the tender skin of a partially feathered nestling. Parents create a sun umbrella by perching on the rim of the nest and spreading their wings.

FLEDGLING The young leave the nest about 10 days after hatching but continue to be fed by Mom and Dad for nearly two more weeks.

JUVENILE The young are mature enough on their return from wintering areas the following spring to nest and raise their own young.

Do the Math

Bulk up! Gray Catbirds increase in muscle and body mass to prepare for fall migration. To muscle their way during long flights, their pectorals, the muscles that power the down flap of flight, increase by nearly one-third. They also need the muscle to carry the extra fat reserves that fuel migration. How much energy? About one and a half times increase in body mass from nonmigratory season!

When

Diurnal. Gray Catbirds are active during the day and rest at night. However, they are one of the few songbirds that sing into the night.

Migration

Spring Arrival: April–May
Fall Departure: Aug–Oct
Short- to mid-distance migrant to southern US or as far south as Panama and the West Indies. They generally travel just far enough south to find fruit from trees and shrubs.

Nesting

Gray Catbirds begin nest construction in May in the Northeast US.

Getting Around

Catbirds maneuver through and just above a thick tangle of shrubs with a combination of hopping and short flights of even wingbeats. During courtship (dating), the male fluffs his feathers and chases an equally fluffed up female.

Where to Look

Look to the scientific name of the Gray Catbird for a clue to their habitat. *Dumetella* means "small thickets" which describes the thick, brushy undergrowth in deciduous forests, edges, parks, backyards and overgrown fields where catbirds nest and find food.

Year-round	Summer
Migration	Winter

Brown Thrasher

Toxostoma rufum

Length: 9–12 inches (23–30 cm)
Wingspan: 11½–12½ inches (29–32 cm)

juvenile

Immature thrashers look similar to the adults but with gray eyes and cream-colored spotting on the upper sides of their bodies

Yellow eye

Rusty colored upper body

Long, slightly curved bill used as a broom to sweep leaves aside and pick up insects

Rusty colored long tail

White underside with streaks of dark brown

Males and females look alike

"Plant a seed, plant a seed, bury it . . ." The male's spring song declares his space and desire for a female.

Beethoven of the Forest

Beethoven, make room. The Brown Thrasher singing a catchy tune of double phrases is an expert composer. Thrashers are their own woodland orchestra, singing more than one note at a time and each note at a different intensity. Birds do not have vocal cords, like you do. A bird's voice box, or syrinx, has two independent chambers. Nerves from the left side of the syrinx stimulate the left chamber while nerves from the right side stimulate the right chamber. This allows the bird to duet with itself. Birds control volume by inflating air sacs that in turn put pressure on the muscles of the syrinx. Brown Thrashers can compose from over 1,000 different musical phrases resulting in more than 2,000 songs!

Habitat Café

Yumm . . . bring an order of grasshoppers, ants, beetles, acorns and berries. Brown Thrashers are omnivorous. They eat plant and animal matter, depending on the season.

SPRING, SUMMER, FALL MENU:
Mainly insects, lots of berries and fruit

WINTER MENU:
Fewer berries and more insects than spring, summer and fall

Life Cycle

NEST The female and male build the twig basket nest 2–5 feet above the ground in the fork of a tree or shrub. At times they will nest on the ground. The basket nest is made in four steps, beginning with a bulky base of twigs and vines woven together, followed by a layer of leaves, and then a layer of small roots, stems and twigs. Lastly, the nest is lined with small grass rootlets that they clean by stomping (thrashing) the dirt off with their feet. A very clean and cozy nest!

EGGS About 1 inch long. The female and male both incubate the clutch of 3–5 eggs for 11–12 days.

MOM! DAD! Altricial. Both parents feed and care for the quickly growing young. In just 9 days the chicks have their feathers.

NESTLING The downy chicks stay in the nest for 11–12 days.

FLEDGLING Parents stay with the young for the first month and bring less food as the young become more independent.

JUVENILE They are ready to date, mate and raise their own young when spring comes around.

Did You Know?

Listen for the repeating phrases for a sure clue that you are tapping in time to the Beethoven of the forest. "Plant-a-seed, plant-a-seed, bury-it, bury-it, cover-it-up, cover-it-up, let-it-grow, let-it-grow, pull-it-up, pull-it-up, eat-it, eat-it, yum-yum, yum-yum." Do Brown Thrashers sing these words? No, people give words to bird sounds to help them remember and identify them. Trek to the woods to listen to their song firsthand and compose your own phrases. Be creative!

When
Brown Thrashers are diurnal, active during the day and resting at night.

Migration
Spring Arrival: Mar–May
Fall Departure: Aug–Oct
They are short-distance migrants moving to the southern United States in the winter, preferring areas that stay above freezing (32 degrees F). Some may remain in the Northeast where they feed on berries and fruits.

Nesting
In the Northeastern US, Brown Thrashers build their nests in May and lay their eggs in May and June.

Getting Around
Brown Thrashers spend most of their time on the ground walking and running after insects and hopping over brush and small trees. Their flight is low to the ground from shrub to shrub. Long, heavy legs are built to kick up leaves from the forest floor.

Where to Look
Shrubby, deciduous forest edges, wooded fence rows, farm windbreaks and wooded parks with open areas.

Year-round	Summer
Migration	Winter

American Robin

Turdus migratorius

Length: 8–11 inches (20–28 cm)
Wingspan: 12–16 inches (31–40 cm)

female

Females not as brightly colored as males

Gray above with very dark head, wings and tail

White eye-ring and white chin

In flight, look for the white between their tummy and tail

Young have speckled breast and white flecks on their dark backs

"Red" breast—brown to dark red-orange

White tips on outer tail feathers

Brown legs

"Cheerily, cheer-up, cheer-up, cheer-up, cheerily, cheer-up!" This cheery song is sung during the time of nesting and incubation.

Squirmy Worms & Super-sized Storage

When you see an American Robin with its head turned to the side and looking with one eye at the ground, it is probably ready to pounce on an insect with its yellow bill. Rather than eat it right away, the robin may store the food in its stretchy esophagus to digest later. Robins eat about 14 feet of earthworms in one day. At this rate, how many feet of earthworms could a robin eat in a week? Do the math (answer on pages 194–195). In the winter, robins pack their esophagus full of berries before the sun goes down. They digest food from this storage space when their body needs a snack before morning. Delicious!

Today's Special

earthworms

Habitat Café

Yumm . . . bring an order of earthworms, beetles, grasshoppers, larvae, crickets, spiders, berries and other fruits. American Robins are omnivorous. They need more protein-rich insects during egg-laying and molting season than in the winter.

SPRING, SUMMER, FALL MENU:
 Mostly fruit and berries, lots of insects

WINTER MENU:
Mainly fruit and berries, some insects

Life Cycle

NEST The female builds the nest in the fork of a tree, on a fence post, a window ledge, or a manmade nesting platform. The outside of the nest is made with dead grass and twigs. To get just the right shape, she uses the bend of her wing and presses from the inside. Next, she carries mud in her bill for the inside. She turns her body in the hollow of the cup for the final fitting. The nest is lined with soft, dead grass.

EGGS About 1 inch long. The female incubates the clutch of 3–4 bright blue eggs for 12–14 days.

MOM! DAD! Altricial. The chicks hatch without feathers. Their skin is so thin that you can see the inside of their tiny bodies.

NESTLING The chick that begs the soonest, stretches its neck the highest and holds it beak closest to the parent gets food first. During the first 10 days, each nestling gets 35–40 feedings per day.

FLEDGLING They leave the nest at about 2 weeks of age and stay on the ground, fed mostly by Dad while Mom prepares for the next brood. Leave fledglings for their parents to care for, and keep your cat inside.

JUVENILE In late August, juveniles form a flock and prepare to migrate south.

Birding Tip

Make a small mud puddle in your backyard. (It's a good idea to ask first.) Watch from afar as a female robin takes mud for building her nest. When you see a mud-covered female, you'll know her nest is nearby. Set out bright colored yarn and string. She may use this in her nest, too!

When

American Robins are diurnal. They feed during the day and rest at night.

Migration

Spring Arrival: Mar–Apr
Fall Departure: Sep–Nov
Short-distance migrant. Winters in southeastern states in areas without snow cover and plenty of food such as fruit from shrubs.

Nesting

American Robins begin nesting in April–May in the Northeastern US. They raise one or two broods each year. Most robins nest within 25 miles of their birthplace.

Getting Around

Robins are speedy, using their sturdy leg muscles to run and hop in the grass. You may see them stop and look around quickly for prey or predators, and then they are off and running again. During migration, robins are fast, straight fliers, with their pointed wings (20–36 mph). They use their medium-length tail for steering through trees during a quick escape.

Where to Look

Most of the Northeastern US in areas with open woods, forest edges, farm windbreaks, parks and backyards.
· *Super Adaptor*

| Year-round | Summer |
| Migration | Winter |

Deciduous Forest Habitat

American Woodcock

Scolopax minor

Length: 10–12 inches (25–31 cm)
Wingspan: 16½–19 inches (42–48 cm)

Juveniles look like dully colored adults; they may have a dark gray band on their throat

Short neck

Long bill is extra sensitive to help find earthworms and soil insects

Disguised in leaf-brown and a feather pattern that looks like dead grass

Short legs

Male and female look alike

Whistling Wings: The sharp whistling comes from air rushing through the three narrow, stiff outer wing feathers.

Romance in the Skies

Romance in the skies requires low light. Go to an open field near a river, bog, or wet area in April–May when the faint light of dawn, dusk, or moonlight casts only a whisper of your shadow—*shh*. Listen for the winged notes of the American Woodcock as he spirals to the moon and flutters to earth in an aerial dance. First, he shows his desire for a female as he struts on the short grass. Then, tail up and spread, he makes a peenting sound (buzz) every few seconds. Suddenly he rises, flying off at an angle in whistling circles ever higher until he reaches 200–300 feet. Like a falling star, he flickers through the sky, landing where he started, and repeats his twilight ballad.

Habitat Café

Yumm . . . bring an order of earthworms with a side of larvae, ants, slugs and snails. American Woodcocks are insectivores. They glean (pick up) insects with their long 2½-inch bill. Eyes are far back on their head so they can see while their bill is in the ground.

SPRING, SUMMER, FALL WINTER MENU:

≈ Mostly earthworms with some insects and snails

Life Cycle

NEST The simple ground nest is a slight depression in the leaves. The female may line the rim of the nest with a few twigs.

EGGS Just over 1 inch long. The female incubates the clutch of 4 eggs for 20–21 days. If the female is flushed from the nest during incubation, she may not return to it. Respect the needs of wildlife.

MOM! DAD! Precocial. The young chicks leave the nest as soon as they hatch. If in danger, they "freeze." Mom feeds the chicks for the first week. Then the young probe for earthworms and insects on their own. They begin to fly after about two weeks of age and are nearly full grown at four weeks.

JUVENILE Juvenile woodcocks set out on their own at 4–6 weeks of age to join with others on fields at night until fall migration. In the Northeast, American Woodcock migration may be as early as August or as late as November.

Did You Know?

A woodcock's bill is designed for pulling worms from the soil. The tips of the mandibles (jaws) can be moved apart while the base of the bill is held together (like a pair of pinchers or tweezers). Stick your pencil in the mud and pull it out. The hole will look like one made by a woodcock. Finding "pencil holes" as you explore the forests is a clue that a woodcock may be near. You might also want to do some research about the woodcock's upside-down brain!

When

Crepuscular. They are active near sunrise and sunset when the light is dim. May feed in daylight.

Migration

Spring Arrival: Mar–Apr
Fall Departure: late Aug–Nov
Short-distance migrant. Migrates by night, low to the ground in small flocks to Tennessee, Arkansas and the Gulf states.

Nesting

American Woodcocks nest in wooded areas near a wet area in the Northeast in April–May.

Getting Around

American Woodcocks walk along the ground with their long bill ahead of them. Look for slender tracks in soft mud with 3 toes forward and 1 short toe backward. They can swim short distances and fly low to the ground in a zig-zag to avoid predators.

Where to Look

Forest and shrub edges with nearby openings, including fields, pastures, northern blueberry barrens, and the moist areas near rivers and bogs.

Year-round	Summer
Migration	Winter

Deciduous Forest Habitat

Mourning Dove

Zenaida macroura

Length: 9–13½ inches (23–34 cm)
Wingspan: 15–18 inches (37–45 cm)

side profile

Small head

Males have a rosy colored breast

Females have a tan breast and brown crown and are smaller than males

Light gray above and buff below with black spot on wing and tail

Young are mottled with white wingtips

Short, red legs and fleshy, red feet

"Coo-oo, OO-OO-OO." The male's call to attract a female. Try this. Blow softly across the neck of an open bottle. It will sound similar to a dove.

Long tail that comes to a point

Cooing All Over the Northeast

Coo-oooo-oo-oo . . . You may wake up to the soothing coos of a love-struck Mourning Dove in New York, Maine, or Connecticut. You may hear the whistle of their wings on a farm in Pennsylvania or farther north in Vermont. Word has it that they have even been heard in Boston and around the monuments in our nation's capital, Washington, D.C. Mourning Doves are Super Adaptors, able to live in many different habitats all over the Northeastern US. As long as they can find seeds to eat and cover to nest in, Mourning Doves will be in our cities, farms, parks and suburban neighborhoods. Spread cracked corn on the ground. A cooing neighbor may come close enough to sketch, photograph, or to simply enjoy their coo . . . mpany.

Habitat Café

Yumm . . . bring an order of seeds. Mourning Doves are herbivores. They eat seeds scattered over short grass and from bird feeders with a perch. At times, they will eat insects. Fill your backyard bird bath; birds need water every day!

SPRING, SUMMER, FALL, WINTER MENU:

 Almost all seeds

Life Cycle

NEST The nest is built in a tree or shrub, in an old nest of another bird such as a robin, on the ledge of a building, or on the ground. Both parents make the flimsy platform nest of twigs and line it with finer twigs.

EGGS About 1¼ inches long. For over two weeks, Dad incubates the 2 eggs during the day and Mom takes the night shift.

MOM! DAD! Altricial. For the first week, Mom and Dad feed the young crop milk. This bird baby formula is a secretion from their crop that has water, nutrients high in vitamins A and B, and a higher protein and fat content than human or cow's milk! Seeds are gradually added at an increasing rate each day.

NESTLING At least one parent stays at the nest at all times.

FLEDGLING Young leave the nest at about two weeks of age. They continue to be fed some seeds by Dad in decreasing amounts until they are about one month of age, when they forage for seeds on their own.

JUVENILE Juveniles flock with other immature doves and move to areas with plentiful food, such as fields of harvested wheat.

Did You Know?

Mourning Doves pick up as many seeds from the ground as their bi-lobed crop will hold. The seeds are digested later in the safety of their nesting and roosting site. A bird's crop is a large sac at the bottom of the esophagus. How many seeds can a Mourning Dove's crop hold? The highest number recorded was over 17,000 bluegrass seeds!

When

Mourning Doves are diurnal. They feed during the day and rest at night.

Migration

Spring Arrival: Apr–May
Fall Departure: Oct–Nov
Short- to mid-distance migrant to central and southern regions of the US. They move south in the cold months because their fleshy feet are easily frostbitten. Some travel as far as Mexico and Costa Rica while some Mourning Doves may overwinter.

Nesting

Mourning Doves begin nesting in the Northeastern US in late April and may continue through August. They raise 1–4 broods per year.

Getting Around

Mourning Doves walk or run on the ground when foraging for food rather than hopping. In flight, Mourning Doves are swift, changing direction and altitude quickly.

Where to Look

Most of the wooded areas of the Northeastern US, except the deep, thick coniferous and deciduous forests. Look for Mourning Doves in your neighborhood!
· *Super Adaptor*

Year-round	Summer
Migration	Winter

Deciduous Forest Habitat

Eastern Screech-Owl

Megascops asio

Length: 6–10 inches (16–25 cm)
Wingspan: 19–24 inches (48–61 cm)

Two color-morphs: gray and rufous (rust)

Ear tufts mimic sticks

Yellow eyes and bill

Male and female look alike, females generally larger

Large feet and feathered toes

Begins calling in February and March. Makes a trill, bark, hoot, rasp, chuckle and "Screech!"

Magicians Among Us

Magicians live in the trees of the Northeast. One may even live near your yard, school, or local park. You will need to learn their magic tricks to find them. Under the veil of darkness they perch on a limb to stalk their next meal. When the light of day materializes, they hide in the chamber of a tree or hollow limb, perhaps staring right at you. Their secret to being invisible? They sit straight up to look like tree bark, raise their ears tufts like tree sticks, squint their eyes to mere slits and hold their feathers and wings tight against their body. If you are very close, they may shift sideways and raise a wing like a cloak of invisibility, covering all but their eyes. Abracadabra!

Habitat Café

Yumm . . . bring an order of songbirds, squirrels, bats, moles, mice, rabbits, snakes, toads, frogs, crayfish, salamanders, beetles, moth larvae, crickets, grasshoppers, cicadas and fish. Eastern Screech-Owls are carnivorous. Active at night, they capture prey with their feet.

SPRING & SUMMER MENU:
 Insects and birds

FALL & WINTER MENU:
 Small mammals

Life Cycle

NEST True recyclers, screech-owls lay their eggs on the former nests of squirrels or other birds in a tree and limb hollows, or a stump. It is 13–20 feet from the ground. The nest floor may have old leaves, rotted wood, or leftovers from previous renters

EGGS About 1½ inch long. The female incubates the clutch of 3–5 eggs for 26–30 days. The male may bring her food.

MOM! DAD! Altricial. The chicks depend on Dad to bring food and Mom to tear it into bite-size pieces.

NESTLING Chicks cooperate in keeping the nest corners for defecation. They practice their first vocals, making eerie trills, hoots and screeches into the night darkness.

FLEDGLING At about four weeks the chicks leave the nest for a nearby limb or tree. Mom and Dad deliver meals for 8–10 weeks while the young practice being predators, pouncing on objects and learning to cache food.

JUVENILE At one year of age, they can nest and raise their own woodland magicians. Poof!

Did You Know?

You can make a simple nest box for screech-owls. Use lumber about ¾ inch thick; 2¾-inch-diameter entrance hole, its bottom 10 inches above floor; front-sloping lid 2 inches above entrance hole, overhanging 1 inch, hinged at back, hooked at side; floor 7 x 7 inches with nail-sized drain holes in bottom corners. Place the box 10–13 feet high on a tree trunk in a shady area about 100 feet from any other owl nest box or cavity. Sprinkle about 1 inch of dry leaf litter on the bottom. Have fun!

When

Nocturnal. Eastern Screech-Owls are active at night (nocturnal) and sometimes at dawn and dusk, called crepuscular.

Migration

Permanent resident. Eastern Screech-Owls stay in the Northeastern US all year.

Nesting

Eastern Screech-Owls in the Northeastern US begin laying their eggs in March–April in nest boxes, the hollow of a tree, or in recycled tree cavities dug out by flickers and woodpeckers.

Getting Around

Screech-Owls fly low through the forest in a steady flight. To disguise where they land, they make a sudden U-turn up to a new perch. To capture prey on the ground, they walk, hop, or run.

Where to Look

Brushy edges and borders of deciduous forests in the Northeastern US. Mature deciduous trees with nesting cavities in places like city parks, backyards, schoolyards, rural woodlots and along rivers and lakes.

Year-round	Summer
Migration	Winter

Deciduous Forest Habitat

Northern Flicker

Colaptes auratus

Length: 11–12 inches (28–31 cm)
Wingspan: 16½–20 inches (42–51 cm)

Long bill

Red patch on gray crown

Male has black mustache

Gray-brown with dark bars on back

Black bib on upper breast

Bright yellow under wings and tail and shaft of flight feathers

White rump patch shows in flights

Male defends space with a loud "wika-wika-wika" and flicks open wings and tail to show his bright underside.

Anteater-on-Wings

What eats the most ants of any North American bird? What member of the woodpecker family rarely pecks? The Northern Flicker. Rather than peck wood out of a tree for a nest hole, Northern Flickers choose a rotten tree and dig out the punky (soft) wood. They generally don't use their bill to peck for food either. Anteaters-on-wings, flickers probe the forest soil with their bill and snap ants up with their 3-inch-long, sticky tongue. Invite flickers by keeping dead trees as wildlife hotels. Build and place nest boxes filled with sawdust too. Once flickers come and nest, you may have long-time lodgers. They often return to the same site each year!

Habitat Café

Yumm . . . bring an order of ants and beetles with side orders of grasshoppers, topped with wild fruits and berries, a few seeds and nuts. Northern Flickers are omnivorous, eating both plant and animal matter. A researcher counted some 5,000 ants in just one flicker!

SPRING & SUMMER MENU:
 Mostly insects with some fruits and berries

FALL, WINTER MENU:
 Berries of trees, shrubs and vines with some insects

Life Cycle

NEST Both the male and female chisel away wood in a dead or dying tree, called a snag. Flickers also use fence posts, poles and nest boxes packed with sawdust. The nest tree is generally located near anthills.

 EGGS About 1 inch long. The clutch of 5–8 eggs is incubated by both parents for about 11–14 days.

MOM! DAD! Altricial. Parents store ant larvae in their crop and deliver this lunch to their young by spitting it back up.

NESTLING A peck on the chick's heel or rump is a signal from Mom and Dad that it is diaper duty time. Parents eat the sacs for the first ten days and carry the sacs away from the nest from then on.

FLEDGLING The young leave the nest when they are nearly four weeks of age and generally in the order that they hatched.

JUVENILE Watch for flicker families filling up on ants near anthills in late summer. At one year old, flickers are able to drum-and-date, mate and raise their own family.

Did You Know?

An important part of the forest ecosystem, flicker nests are recycled by American Kestrels and some ducks. European Starlings are a different matter. They will barge into an active flicker nest, take out the eggs and set up house. Red squirrels will kill young flickers in the nest. Buzzzzzz . . . beware. When threatened, young flickers mimic the sound of a swarm of bees. So long, predators!

When

Diurnal. Flickers are active during the day and rest at night.

Migration
Spring Arrival: Apr
Fall Departure: Sep–Oct.
Short-distance migrant flying mostly by night to areas in the southern Atlantic coastal states. Some flickers may overwinter.

Nesting
Flickers begin egg laying in May in the Northeastern US in areas with dead and dying trees or in nest boxes.

Flickers defend their breeding and nesting territory by drumming on objects that offer the most bang for their efforts: trees, poles and metal objects.

Getting Around
Flickers hop when on the ground, on a tree or limb. Like most members of the woodpecker family, their flight is up-and-down, called undulating. The stiff tail is used as a prop when drumming on a tree.

Where to Look
Forest edges and open woodlands bordering fields.

Year-round	Summer
Migration	Winter

Deciduous Forest Habitat

Cooper's Hawk

Accipiter cooperii

Length: 14½–15½ inches (37–39 cm)
Wingspan: 24½–35½ inches (62–90 cm)

soaring

Red eyes

Gray above; underside is white with rust-colored bars

Short, rounded wings for cruising around trees

juvenile

Immature: yellow eyes; brown back with brown streaks on breast and belly

Females are ⅓ larger than the males

Long gray tail with black bands and a white tip

"Cak-cak-cak!" This call is given by males and females when the nest is in danger or the bird is excited.

Small Birds Beware—Accipiter in the Area!

The eyes have it. Cooper's Hawks have eyes so large there is little room left in their skull to move them. Hawks move their entire head from side to side and up and down to get a full range of vision. They are equipped with a monocle, a pair of binoculars and a telescope! Monocular vision allows each eye to see a separate image. The bird can scan and search for prey. Once located, binocular vision (both eyes seeing forward) allows the bird to judge the distance and depth of moving prey. Telescopic vision then allows the hawk to zero in on prey by making the image larger. Small birds beware—a Cooper's Hawk with eyes nearly as large as its stomach may be spying on you!

Habitat Café

Yumm . . . bring an order of Mourning Doves, robins, Blue Jays, starlings, chipmunks, rabbits, squirrels and mice with a side of frog. Cooper's Hawks are carnivorous. During nesting season, prey may be cached in a roost tree.

SPRING, SUMMER, FALL, WINTER MENU:

 Mainly birds, with a few mammals, reptiles, amphibians and insects

Life Cycle

NEST The male and female build the bulky twig and stick nest 20–60 feet high in a deciduous or coniferous tree. The 2-foot-wide nest is lined with small chips or flakes of bark.

EGGS About 2 inches long. The female incubates the clutch of 4–5 eggs for 24–36 days.

MOM! DAD! Altricial. Mom broods the young for the first two weeks. She spreads her wings as an umbrella.

NESTLING Dad brings the food and Mom tears the prey into bite-sized pieces. Parents carry away food pellets and uneaten food. Diaper duty? Not in this nest. The young are able to scoot to the rim of the nest and take care of this stinky job on their own.

FLEDGLING The young leave the nest when they are about one month old. Mom and Dad continue to bring food for nearly two more months.

JUVENILE At two years of age they are ready to date, mate and raise their own young.

Do the Math

In a study of a Cooper's Hawk nest, researchers found that it took an average of 66 robin-sized prey to raise one young hawk to the age of six weeks. How many prey would parent hawks need to capture for a family of three chicks over six weeks? Four chicks? Five chicks? Where do they find prey? Watch your bird feeders for a Cooper's Hawk shopping for a meal—and they do not eat bird seeds or suet! Answer on pages 194–195.

When

Cooper's Hawks are diurnal. They feed during the day and rest at night.

Migration

Spring Arrival: Apr–May
Fall Departure: Sep–Oct
Short- to mid-distant migrant following the Atlantic coastline and mountainous ridges to the southern United States, Mexico and Central America.

Nesting

Cooper's Hawks begin nesting in late March–April.

Getting Around

Cooper's Hawks fly low to the ground in a series of fast wing beats and then a swift glide. Gliding saves energy, and uses $\frac{1}{20}$ the energy of normal flight.

Where to Look

Deciduous and mixed deciduous-coniferous forests, often near a river or lake. They hunt along forested edges.

Year-round	Summer
Migration	Winter

Deciduous Forest Habitat

Barred Owl

Strix varia

Length: 17–20 inches (43–50 cm)
Wingspan: 39–43 inches (99–110 cm)

landing

Yellow beak

Dark blue eyes surrounded by facial disc that looks like huge glasses

Young look like the adults

Gray-brown with bars across its breast

Brown downward streaks on the pale belly

Females and males look alike with females generally larger

"Who cooks for you, who cooks for you all?" Most common in February—early March in the Northeast.

Of Friend and Foe

Barred Owls and Red-shouldered Hawks hang out in the same habitat. They have an understanding. This is not the case between Barred Owls and Great Horned Owls. In small forest spaces and broken-up forests, Barred Owls move out when Great Horned Owls move in. Why? Great Horned Owls kill Barred Owls. They kill the young Barred Owls in the nest, young that have just left the nest, and even adults. In larger forested areas, all is well. Each species has enough space to spread out and establish territories and there is a greater supply of food. Friend or foe? Habitat is the key.

Today's Special
mice

Habitat Café

Yumm . . . bring an order of small mammals, a few small birds, and a couple reptiles and amphibians. Barred Owls are carnivorous. They will hang around bird feeders to catch the mice and voles that are attracted to fallen seed on the ground.

SPRING, SUMMER, FALL, WINTER MENU:

 Mostly mammals, some birds, reptiles, amphibians and insects

Life Cycle

NEST Barred Owls use a hollow tree cavity or an old hawk, crow, heron, or squirrel nest in the top of a tall tree. The recycled nest may be lined with some of their own feathers. They will also use a nesting box.

EGGS About 2 inches long. The female incubates the clutch of 2–3 eggs for 28–33 days.

MOM! DAD! Altricial. As soon as they hatch, the white fuzz balls call and beg for food. Dad hunts and Mom tears the food into soft bite-sized pieces. She stays at the nest for most of the first two weeks, warming the chicks until their larger feathers grow in.

NESTLING Starting after the third week, Dad leaves prey in the nest while Mom is gone. They learn to tear apart their own dinner.

FLEDGLING The young leave the nest still unable to fly when they are 4–5 weeks old and perch on a branch as they wait for Mom and Dad to bring food. Flying lessons begin when they are 10 weeks of age.

JUVENILE Mom and Dad bring food until early fall, when the teens move away to establish their own spaces. They are mature enough to date, mate and raise their own young when they are 2 years old.

Did You Know?

Our ears do not hear the full range of sounds that birds make. How do we know? We can see the bird sounds that we hear and don't hear on an electric sonogram. When you hear echoes in the forest darkness that send your imagination into overdrive, this may be a pair of Barred Owls "jiving," a duet of hoots, caws, cackles and gurgles. All this ruckus to impress and bond to each other. Of course, they sleep during the day!

When

Nocturnal, active during the night and resting during the day. Hunting is done mostly right after dark and just before dawn.

Migration

Permanent resident: Barred Owls live all year in the Northeastern US.

Nesting

Barred Owls get an early wing up on the nesting season. They begin to nest and lay eggs as early as March in the Northeastern US.

Getting Around

Barred Owls perch in trees to listen and watch for movement of prey below. Once alerted to prey, the owl drops like a bullet on silent wings to snatch its target. They have flight paths they use routinely through their territory.

Where to Look

Mature (older) deciduous and mixed deciduous-coniferous forests in the Northeastern US.

Year-round	Summer
Migration	Winter

Deciduous Forest Habitat

Great Horned Owl

Bubo virginianus

Length: 18–25 inches (46–63 cm)
Wingspan: 3–5 feet (101–145 cm)

Very large, yellow eyes

Hooked beak to tear the muscles and bones of prey

Females are heavier and larger than males

Ear tufts; only large Northeastern owl with long, feathered ear tufts

in flight

Facial disc of feathers funnel sound waves to their ears for extraordinary hearing

spitting pellet

Both males and females have brown, black and cream lines over most of their body, with a white bib

"Who-hoo-ho-oo?" or, "This is my territory." Hooting duets between paired males and females can be heard from January until the first eggs are laid.

Flying Mousetrap

The hooting of Great Horned Owls can wake you up just about any season and anywhere in the Northeast, whether you are tucked under your winter covers or watching summer fireflies light your room. Winter is the best time to listen for owls, but I've been driven to giggles on summer nights listening to young owls practicing their whooing. *Super Adaptors*, they live in cities, rural farming areas and places in between. They need a large tree for nesting and plenty of mice, rabbits, squirrels and skunks for the taking. The full menu includes stray cats and animals as large as porcupines! Hear a Great Horned Owl in the night and know that this flying mousetrap is hard at work in your neighborhood.

oday's Special

pet cats—
keep "Kitty"
indoors!

Habitat Café

Yumm . . . bring an order of mice, rabbits, hares, ground squirrels, muskrats, squirrels, pocket gophers, snakes, small birds, pheasants, ducks and geese. They may take animals as large as raccoons, skunks, porcupines, or Great Blue Herons. Great Horned Owls are carnivorous.

SPRING, SUMMER, FALL, WINTER MENU:
 Mostly mammals, a few birds

Life Cycle

NEST These big owls do not make their own nest. They use a hollow tree cavity or an old hawk, crow, heron, or squirrel nest in the top of a tall tree. Owls may line the recycled nest with some of their own feathers. They will also nest in a man-made nest base.

EGGS About 2 inches long. The female incubates the clutch of 2–3 eggs for 28–33 days. She does not leave the eggs for more than a few minutes at a time to keep them from freezing.

MOM! DAD! Altricial. Cold, wind and snow mean that Mom broods the young downy chicks for the first three weeks. Dad brings food. As feathers replace the down, Mom leaves to hunt too.

NESTLING Able to feed themselves at about four weeks of age.

FLEDGLING At six weeks of age, young owls venture out to nearby branches. Their first test flights begin the following week.

JUVENILE Teenage owls stay with their parents during the summer and set out to find their own territories in late fall and early winter. At 2 years of age, they are able to mate and raise their own young.

Gross Factor

What does an owl do with the bones and fur of their eaten prey? It forms them into a pellet and spits them back up. You'll know you're under an owl roost when you find gray, 2–3-inch pellets. Break open a compact pellet and you may discover the tiny bones of a mouse, the jawbone of a rabbit, spine sections of a gopher, or the beak of a starling, all surrounded by undigested fur.

When

Nocturnal. Feeds at night and rests during the day. At times, they will hunt during the day.

Migration

Permanent resident. Stays all year in the Northeastern US. Many predators fly south for the winter, leaving Great Horned Owls to take advantage of less competition for prey.

Nesting

One of the earliest nesting birds in the Northeastern US, it begins nesting in February. This adaptation may provide them with enough time for the young to mature and lets them take advantage of greater food availability.

Getting Around

Silent flight. An extra fuzzy covering over the flight feathers quiets the rush of air over the short, wide, powerful wings. It tucks its head in and holds its wings straight out, alternating strong wingbeats with glides. On the ground, it walks in alternating steps.

Where to Look

Look for Great Horned Owls in open areas, perched on poles, fence posts, trees and rock outcrops scanning for food.
· *Super Adaptor*

Year-round	Summer
Migration	Winter

Deciduous Forest Habitat

Wild Turkey

Meleagris gallopavo

Length: 3–4 feet (110–115 cm)
Wingspan: 4–5 feet (125–144 cm)

non-displaying male

female

Hens wear dull brown camouflage

Broad, rounded wings and tail; toms (males) have a tail that spreads into a large fan

Bare red and blue head and neck with wattle (bumpy skin under the chin that puffs out)

Male: Long black beard; modified feather tufts 9 inches or more

Body or contour feathers are broad and squared on the ends

"Gobble, gobble!" or, "This is my territory! Males stay away. Females come over!"

Long legs, with spur on back—both males and females have spurs, but only the young males' grow into pointed and curved spurs up to 2 inches long

Tree Houses for Turkeys

When the sun sinks low and the shadows are long, look up in the trees for Wild Turkeys as they move from limb to limb to settle in for the night. They roost alone or in groups in the deciduous trees of the Northeast. Tucking in for a snooze, they rest their chest on a limb and lock their long toes around it—for support. Then, they place their head over their back and beneath their unusually long humeral (back) feathers. Sleep tight, zzzzz . . . The morning sun is greeted with "tree yelps" from the waking turkeys and perhaps a round of "gobble, gobble, gobble" from the males. It's time to hit the forest floor for a fresh breakfast of acorns, hickory nuts and berries.

Habitat Café

Yumm . . . bring an order of buds, ferns, bugs, seeds, fruit, grass, nuts (acorns), field grains and more. Wild Turkeys are omnivorous.

SPRING, SUMMER, MENU:
 Fruit, berries, insects and plants

FALL MENU:
Acorns and hickory nuts

WINTER MENU:
Corn and other grains from fields

Life Cycle

NEST The female builds the nest in dead leaves on the ground, often hidden under a log, in a bush, or at the base of a tree. She lines the nest depression with dry leaves. Mom camouflages the nest and eggs with more leaves when she takes a recess from incubation.

 EGGS About 2½ inches long. The female incubates the clutch of 8–15 eggs for 27–28 days. Dad is busy grouping up with his harem of several females.

MOM! DAD! Precocial and downy. The newly hatched chicks leave the nest within one day of hatching. Mom leads them to food where they feed on protein-rich insects, seeds and berries. For warmth and protection from predators, the chicks nestle under Mom's wing. The young birds have their wing feathers and can fly at two weeks of age. They fly up to a nearby tree branch where they spend the night roosting.

JUVENILE The brood stays together until winter when several hens and their broods join together in a large flock. Toms and jakes (young males) form their own flocks.

Gross Factor

How do you know if you are on the trail of a tom or hen? Scat (excrement). Yes, male and female turkeys leave different scat. Males, or toms, leave a J-shaped scat over ⅜ inch in diameter. Females, or hens, leave a curly clump less than ⅜ inch in diameter. Look also for the tracks of wild turkeys that are typically 4–5 inches long and 4¼–5¼ inches wide. Turkeys use their feet to uncover insects, acorns and field corn. Look for scratch marks in the snow, too.

When

Wild Turkeys are diurnal, active during the day, feeding in the early morning and afternoon, and resting in trees at night.

Migration

Permanent resident. Wild Turkeys stay in the Northeastern US all year.

Nesting

Wild Turkey males begin gobbling in late February to early March and nesting begins in April in the Northeastern US.

Getting Around

Wild Turkeys are built for a quick get-away rather than a marathon. They fly straight up then away, hard and fast through the treetops at speeds of up to 55 mph over short distances on their rounded wings. They can also run 18 mph for short distances on their long and powerful legs.

Where to Look

Forested areas near open farm fields, wooded areas near rivers, and brushy grasslands in the Northeastern US.

Year-round	Summer
Migration	Winter

Deciduous Forest Habitat

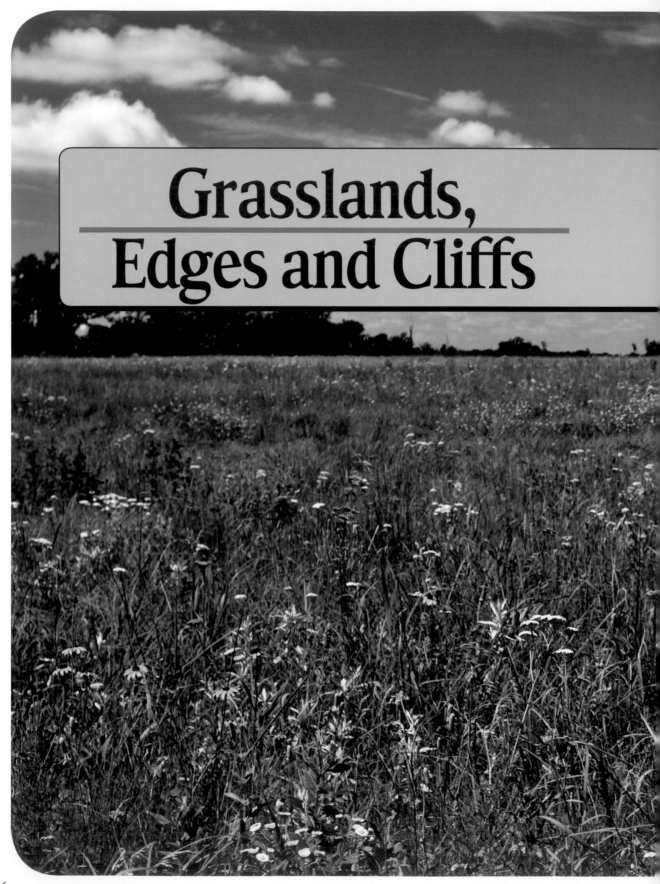

Grasslands, Edges and Cliffs

Skyrocketing from a cliff or snatching insects from a perch at the edge of an open field, birds that live in the margins of grasslands and open spaces are captivating. The Northeastern United States provides valuable habitat for the fastest bird in the world, and more. Turn the pages to get to know these birds firsthand.

Open Sky and Land

The habitat margins of open sky and land are home to hardy and spectacular birds. Some birds living in open areas have adapted to

Fragmented grasslands

small niches along roadsides and field margins while others need large unbroken grasslands, pastures, or hayfields to survive.

In the wide-open areas of grass and field, Northern Harriers perform aerial dances and food exchanges as precise as circus acrobats. Perched on a hayfield fence post, a black-bibbed Eastern Meadowlark rehearses his flute-like whistles. He hopes the area females are wowed, awed and rendered totally chirpless.

Where grassland and forest meet, Eastern Bluebirds snatch insects from open fields to deliver to hungry chicks in a nearby tree cavity or man-made nest box. Brown-headed Cowbirds spy nearby for nests of other bird species in which to secretly deposit their eggs —perhaps even that of a bluebird, Song Sparrow, or Bobolink.

Cliffs and Urban Ledges

Peregrine Falcons hang out on the edges of cliffs in the White Mountains, Adirondacks and Atlantic coast, and, just as comfortably, from downtown cliff-like buildings and from bridges over large rivers like the Hudson and Delaware. Swooping and chipping in urban skies are Chimney Swifts, their bills held wide open to capture insects like a neighborhood patrol.

White Mountains cliffs

The Peregrine Falcon's small cousin, the American Kestrel has also adapted to nest boxes and life in metro areas. The kestrel's accessibility to grasslands around urban areas for foraging is key. Their numbers were steady in metro areas until recently when they took a marked decline. At the same time, Cooper's Hawk numbers have been steadily increasing in urban and suburban areas due to bird feeders and residential areas that now have evergreen trees large enough to provide the woodland hawks with nest sites. American Kestrels may have become an a la carte menu for Cooper's Hawks while the urban grasslands they depend on are disappearing.

Pittsburgh, PA

Land use changes over the past 200 years have altered the Northeastern landscape. Forests were cleared to make way for crop fields and pastures. As a result, this opened the habitat for birds that live in grasslands and near forest edges. In time these open areas have been built upon, replanted, or fragmented into smaller and smaller parcels until the survival of the dependent birds is now in question. Trek to the open spaces and get to know the wildlife. Then, use your new understanding to support and create spaces shared by people and wildlife.

Incredible Critters

Plants and animals that inhabit open areas and margins have adaptations to survive the harsh conditions of the summer heat and the cold and snow of Northeastern winters. American Goldfinches don't migrate south with other birds. They put on a coat of extra feathers and stay for the winter, feeding in large flocks. American Kestrels scan the roadsides until snow covers the ground and then head farther south to find prey. Public areas and those managed by private organizations, such as The Nature Conservancy, are great places to spy on birds.

American Goldfinch in winter plumage

You can also find birds along the margins of roadsides and field edges across most of the region. For up-to-date information on where to find birds in your area check out the Ornithologists' Union and Audubon Club in your state; most sponsor field trips, educational programs and breaking news on the locations of resident and migratory birds. Head outdoors. Wildlife is waiting for you in the open spaces and habitat edges of the Northeastern US!

Check Off the Grasslands Birds You See!

American Goldfinch

Carduelis tristis

Length: 4–5 inches (11–13 cm)
Wingspan: 7½–8½ inches (19–22 cm)

male winter

female

Females are olive-green
with pale yellow chest and
throat, and no black cap

Black cap

The male is bright
yellow in summer,
olive-green in winter

White rump

Black tail
is notched

"Po-ta-to-chip!"
means "This is my space!"
(Sounds like a squeeze-toy.) ♪

Leap-Frogging Goldfinch

Cold, wind, ice and snow send many birds packing their feathers and heading south for the winter. They are looking for warmth and food. American Goldfinches stay. They have adapted to chilly winters and the change from the large food supply of summer to a limited winter store of seeds. In fact, they can make winter feeding look like a group game. Taking turns in leap-frog fashion over mass seed sources is an efficient (energy-saving and safe) way for goldfinches to feed in large winter flocks. This rolling motion over a field helps to protect the flock from predators. Your turn!

Habitat Café

Yumm . . . bring an order of thistle seed and spring tree buds peppered with aphids. Fill your backyard bird feeder with Nyjer thistle seed. American Goldfinches are omnivorous. They use their cone-shaped bill to break open seeds.

SPRING, SUMMER, FALL, WINTER MENU:

 Mostly seeds, a few insects

Life Cycle

NEST The female builds the cup-shaped nest, 2–20 feet above the ground in the fork of a thistle, a shrub, or a deciduous tree. With spider silk, she weaves a nest base to the support branches. Next, rootlets are woven in. Soft thistle down is added last. The nest is so compact (tight), it can hold water like a cup!

EGGS Almost ¾ inch long. The female incubates the 4–6 eggs for 12–14 days. The male feeds her regurgitated (spit-up) food from his crop. Gross, but it works!

MOM! DAD! Altricial. Both mom and dad feed the young. For the first four days Dad feeds Mom, and then she feeds the chicks.

NESTLING Feathers replace the chick's down when they are about one week old, nearly the time they are ready to leave the nest.

FLEDGLING Young goldfinches continue to be cared for by the male for three more weeks. They can then forage for seeds on their own.

JUVENILE Juveniles have feather color and pattern similar to an adult female. They group with other goldfinches and move to areas with plenty of food. In one year, they can nest and raise their own chicks.

Did You Know

Most parent birds feed their young a diet of high-protein insects. American Goldfinches feed seeds to their young. When Brown-headed Cowbirds lay their eggs in the nest of a goldfinch, the cowbird chicks die (for more about cowbird habits, see page 126). The seed diet does not have enough protein for cowbird chicks to live. The goldfinch chicks then have the full attention of their parents.

When

The American Goldfinch is diurnal. It feeds during the day and rests at night.

Migration

Permanent resident to short-distance migrant. The American Goldfinch may move to central and southern regions of the US during harsh winters. Many stay in the Northeastern US during the winter as year-round back-yard visitors.

Nesting

One of the Northeast's latest nesting birds, goldfinches begin nesting in July when the thistle and milkweed down are mature and fluffy.

Getting Around

The male flies in spiral circles over the nesting area. He sings his most impressive 'po-ta-to-chip.' Two or three males join, each circling in crisscross paths like fluttering bright-yellow butterflies. Biologists call this behavior a Butterfly Flight Pattern.

Where to Look

Open grassland, rural fields, shrub edges and backyards throughout most of the North-eastern US.

| Year-round | Summer |
| Migration | Winter |

Grasslands, Edges and Cliff Habitat

Song Sparrow

Melospiza melodia

Length: 4½–6½ inches (12–17 cm)
Wingspan: 7–9½ inches (18–24 cm)

Conical bill for eating seeds

Brown with gray and black streaks above

Large brown spot on chest

White underneath with black and brown streaks

Males are larger than females

"Sweet, sweet, sweet." The male declares his territory or attracts a female with 2–3 identical notes and then a cheery jumble.

Uno, 4M and the Backyard Science of Margaret Morse Nice

On a spring day in 1928, Margaret Morse Nice met Uno and 4M, two male Song Sparrows having a territory battle in her Ohio backyard. Margaret was determined to watch Uno for several hours each day to discover exactly what he did and how he did it. What followed changed the basic understanding of one of the most common sparrows in North America. She discovered that the males sang about 260 songs per hour and that each male had his own unique variation of the species' song pattern. Margaret trailed and documented generations of Song Sparrows in her neighborhood for 14 years—she was hooked! Some of the facts on these pages are the result of her discoveries. Thank you, Margaret.

Today's Special

ants
cracked corn/
millet
BIRD FEEDER TREAT

Habitat Café

Yumm . . . bring an order of insects and seeds with a side order of fresh fruit and berries. Song Sparrows are omnivorous; they eat both plant and animal matter.

SPRING & SUMMER MENU:
Mostly insects and other small invertebrates

FALL & WINTER MENU:
Mostly seeds and fruit, some insects

When
Diurnal. Song Sparrows are active during the day and rest at night.

Migration
Spring Arrival: Mar–Apr
Fall Departure: Sep–Oct
Short-distant migrant to snow-free wintering areas in the southeastern US. Some may overwinter in the Northeastern US.

Nesting
Song Sparrows begin nest construction in April in the Northeastern US. They may raise 1-3 broods per season.

Life Cycle

NEST The female builds the open nest cup on the ground hidden in grasses or a low shrub. She weaves an outer basket with grass, weed stems, leaves and strips of bark. It is lined with fine grass.

EGGS About ¾ inch long. The clutch of 3–5 eggs is incubated by the female for about 12–13 days. When Brown-headed Cowbirds (page 126) are in the area, the nest of the Song Sparrow is often host to their eggs. When a cowbird is at or near the nest, Song Sparrows may stop building and abandon the nest, or send the cowbird packing.

MOM! DAD! Altricial. Parents feed the chicks insects like spiders and aphids and eat or remove the fecal sacs (the chicks' diapers).

NESTLING The chicks have a fast growth spurt in their first week—they grow feathers, open their eyes, stand up, and start to beg for food.

FLEDGLING They leave the nest at about 8–10 days of age but are dependent on their parents for another 2–3 weeks. The young learn to find food, preen, sunbathe, sing, hop, walk, fly, land and defend their area.

JUVENILE They are mature enough on their return the following spring to nest and raise their own young.

Getting Around
Song Sparrows make a short, flitting, direct and low flight between perches in low trees or shrubs. They run when on the ground and sometimes walk with a skip.

Where to Look
In the Northeastern US, Song Sparrows are found mostly in shrubby edges and open habitats often near water, including tidal marshes, freshwater wetlands, fields, pastures, lake and forest edges, roadsides and even city parks and backyards.
· Super Adaptor

Year-round   Summer
Migration   Winter

Unsolved Mystery

Try this backyard science. Find a Song Sparrow in your neighborhood and follow it, just as Margaret Morse Nice did. Take note of how many times and where the bird sings, its behavior and interactions with other birds. Can you tell a difference in the songs of individual Song Sparrows? Return to watch the bird—is it in the same area? Can you tell where its territory begins and ends by watching territory battles? Try this with backyard birds like wrens and robins. Explore the outdoors!

Grasslands, Edges
and Cliff Habitat

Savannah Sparrow

Passerculus sandwichensis

Length: 4½–6 inches (11–15 cm)
Wingspan: 8–9 inches (20–22 cm)

Gray bill

Crown has pale stripe in the middle

Throat and belly are white

Yellow eyebrow stripe

Neck, nape, back and rump are brown-gray with streaks

The streaked breast has a dark spot in the center

Male and female look alike

Pink legs

"Buzzz." Males sing a short, insect-like buzzing song during breeding season to attract a gal.

Scamper, Crouch, Zigzag and Chase

Savannah Sparrow survival lessons may follow like this: In your five flight plans the main pattern is short, low and rapid. Use this to patrol your territory. When in danger employ the drop-to-the-ground tactic. Then, with both wings raised, scamper zigzag along the ground. In all other ground action, crouch and imitate a mouse. Parents, approach the nest with a direct flight and hover before swiftly dropping to the nest. Guys, guard the nest at all cost and use your flutter flight to threaten intruders. Keep your legs dangling, tail cocked at 45° and wings beating in a constant flutter. If a predator is another male Savannah Sparrow, open full bore and chase it with all you have!

Habitat Café

Yumm... bring an order of insects and a small fruit salad sprinkled with seeds. Savannah Sparrows are omnivorous. Using its strong beak, the sparrow crushes an insect and shakes or strikes it against the ground. It then swallows a non-squirmy meal.

SPRING, SUMMER, MENU:
 Mostly insects

FALL, WINTER MENU:
Small seeds, fruits, some insects

Life Cycle

NEST The female builds the 3-inch-diameter cup nest on the ground hidden in tall, dead grasses. The outer shell has coarse grass and the inner shell is made of soft, fine grass.

EGGS About ¾ inch long. The female incubates the clutch of 2–6 (4 average) eggs for 14–16 days.

MOM! DAD! Altricial. During the chicks early 8-day growth spurt, Mom needs to eat nearly 10 times her body mass to keep pace. It takes a great deal of energy to catch and carry family meals. She can multi-task and carry 10-20 small prey (midges) in a trip, but caterpillars have to be carried one by one.

NESTLINGS Both parents help with diaper duty and provide insects and spiders for the chicks' bottomless appetites.

FLEDGLING At 11-12 days of age, the young leave the nest.

JUVENILE Before their first migration, they group into loose flocks of just 3-8 individuals or into a party of 100. Let the feathers fly!

Unsolved Mystery

How do Savannah Sparrows determine their nightly flight route during fall and spring migration? The setting sun is the GPS (Global Positioning System) for these grassland sparrows. It is used as a source of day-to-day mapping information. This information may be then transferred to the stars as celestial reference points each night. This is only one answer. Bird migration still has mysteries just waiting to be solved.

When

Diurnal. Savannah Sparrows are active during the day and rest at night.

Migration

Spring Arrival: Apr
Fall Departure: Sep–Oct
Short- to mid-distance migrant to central and southern United States and as far south as Mexico and Honduras.

Nesting

Savannah Sparrows begin nesting in May–June in the Northeastern US.

Getting Around

Savannah Sparrows walk on the ground to capture prey. Their main foes include the stealthy Northern Harriers and American Kestrels. The sparrow's darting flight is followed by a sudden dive for cover into tall grasses.

Where to Look

Grasslands, hayfields and pastures, meadows, coastal dunes and heaths, edges of salt marshes and grassy marshes.

Year-round   Summer
Migration   Winter

Grasslands, Edges and Cliff Habitat

Bobolink

Dolichonyx oryzivorus

Length: 6–8 inches (15–21 cm)
Wingspan: 10½ inches (27 cm)

female

Female is buff colored with streaks down her back, wings and sides

Juveniles look like females without streaks on the side and more yellow underneath

The male wears a backwards tuxedo; his black belly, wings and head are set off by white on his back; he is also nick-named the "skunk bird"

Stiff, pointed tail feathers

"Bob-o-link, bob-o-link, sspink, spank, sspink." "Males, this is my space. Gals, come over."

Drawing the Line

Male Bobolinks decide where their space (territory) begins and the neighboring male's space ends by doing a boogie called the "Parallel Walk." First they show off their most colorful marking, the yellow patch on the back of the neck. They turn their head down and to the side. Next, the two neighbors hop side by side along an invisible line. This boogie-woogie can go on for hours. "Hey, you're on my side of the line!" Reminds me of the invisible line my sister had down the middle of the back seat in the family car.

Today's Special
caterpillars

Habitat Café

Yumm . . . bring an order of spiders, beetles, grasshoppers and crickets. Bobolink's are omnivorous. As they migrate, Bobolinks eat large amounts of grain in the "milk" stage. This creates body fat (energy reserves) for the long flight south.

SPRING, SUMMER, FALL MENU:
Mainly insects, lots of seeds and grains

WINTER MENU:
Almost all seeds and grains, some insects

Life Cycle

NEST The female builds the nest in an open field. She picks up grasses and builds them around a low area on the ground. Next, she lines the nest with soft, fine grasses.

EGGS About ¾ inch long. The female incubates the 5–6 eggs for 12–13 days.

MOM! DAD! Altricial. Mom does most of the parenting. Dad has up to four hungry families full of hatchlings at the same time.

NESTLING The newly hatched chicks are naked. They grow feathers by the time they are 10 days old and leave the nest.

FLEDGLING Feathers that are the same color as the ground help hide the fledglings in a field or prairie. They can fly on their own at about 2 weeks of age. They beg for food from their parents until they are 3–4 weeks old.

JUVENILE Juveniles join in a flock with their family group and get ready for fall migration. When they return in the spring, they are mature enough to date, mate and raise their own young.

Did You Know?

Eggs are laid one per day over 5–6 days, but all hatch within a day or two of each other. Biologists designed experiments to find out how the eggs might be different depending on what day in the line-up they were laid. Eggs laid last had more of a body chemical called testosterone than the eggs laid first. Higher levels of testosterone cause faster growth and more aggressiveness, helping the chicks from the last eggs catch up!

When

Bobolinks are diurnal. They are active during the day and rest at night.

Migration
Spring Arrival: Apr–May
Fall Departure: Aug–Oct
Long-distance migrant. The Bobolink makes one of the longest migrations of any North American songbird, winging deep into South America, where it spends the winter in the "pampas" grass of Brazil and Argentina—it's an 11,000-mile round trip!

Nesting
Bobolinks begin nesting in the Northeastern US in May–June.

Getting Around
Bobolinks walk slowly while pecking seeds and insects. Flight during nesting season is fast and low, to keep out of the sight of hungry predators. Long hind toenails allow Bobolinks to perch on plant stems.

Where to Look
Open grassland and rural fields. Prefer native grasslands but have adapted to hay fields of at least 1–5 acres in size.

Year-round   Summer
Migration   Winter

Grasslands, Edges and Cliff Habitat   119

Chimney Swift

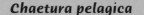
Chaetura pelagica

Length: 5–6 inches (12–15 cm)
Wingspan: 10½–12 inches (27–30 cm)

in flight

Dark gray
compact bird

Male and female
look similar

Toe claws and tail
bristles are used to
cling to rough vertical
surfaces

Short tail tipped
with bristles

"Yip, yip, yip."
Once this high-pitched sound
is heard from the chimney,
the vocal young are about 10
days from flying from the
nest area.

Long tapered
wings cross over
the tail feathers

Eating on the Wing

Fast food takes on a new meaning when it comes to Chimney Swifts. Driven by the need for food on the wing, they are in continual flight, eating nearly one-third of their own body weight in flying insects such as mosquitoes, flies and termites in one day. Chimney Swifts follow flying insects where they are the most plentiful. In morning and late evening they hunt near the ground. During the day they hunt on warm air currents higher in the air. A whirling mass of migrating Chimney Swifts descending for their evening roost can look like a tornado swirling into a chimney. Home owners can relax: Swifts are safe allies to have around. They are also protected by state wildlife codes and federal law.

Today's Special
bees

Habitat Café

Yumm . . . bring an order of flying insects, including leafhoppers, caddis flies, mayflies, crane flies, beetles, wasps, ants and bees. Chimney Swifts are insectivores. Eating can be a group affair with 3–12 swifts, or a dine-alone event during the breeding season. Adults carry food for chicks in a ball, called a bolus, and then cough it up and into the chicks gaping mouth.

SPRING, SUMMER, FALL, WINTER MENU:
Flying insects

Life Cycle

NEST Their natural habitat is a cave or hollow tree. They also nest in chimneys and walls of abandoned buildings. Both parents build a semi-circular nest with the ends of dead twigs that they snap from trees with their feet as they fly, called twigging. The twigs are woven and glued together with saliva and attached to the chimney wall.

EGGS About ¾ inch long. The clutch of 4–5 eggs is incubated by both parents for about 19–20 days.

MOM! DAD! Altricial. The chicks hatch featherless, blind and with long claws to help them cling to the side of the nest. Other adults may help the parents incubate the eggs, brood and feed the nestlings.

NESTLING The young exercise their wings by hanging on the chimney wall and fluttering. They roost together, covering their siblings' backs with their wings.

FLEDGLING They leave the nest cavity at one month of age.

JUVENILE Small groups move to staging chimneys. They migrate to wintering areas in a flock of up to 10,000 birds. They are mature enough on their spring return to mate and nest.

Did You Know?

Chimney Swift numbers are on the decline. Large, hollow nesting trees have become fewer, and once-available chimneys are being replaced by newer building styles. You can take action to provide for Chimney Swifts by identifying and preserving large, hollow trees and by building and maintaining an artificial nesting and roosting chimney. Join the North American Chimney Swift Nest Site Research Project and become a research associate. Find building plans at http://www.chimneyswifts.org/.

When
Diurnal. Chimney Swifts are active during the day and rest at night.

Migration
Spring Arrival: Apr–May
Fall Departure: Aug–Oct
Long-distant migrant during the day in flocks of 100 or more to the upper Amazon basin of South America: Peru, Ecuador, Chile and Brazil.

Nesting
Chimney Swifts begin nest construction in May–June in the Northeastern US.

Getting Around
Hanging onto chimneys and tree cavities requires special feet and toes. In Chimney Swifts, toes 1 and 4 can turn both forward and backward. They can shift all 4 toes forward to use their feet as hooks while roosting. During twigging, they use toes 1 and 2 against toes 3 and 4 to grip and snap off the ends of dead branches. Their flight is fast with twittery wingbeats. They also soar.

Where to Look
In the Northeastern US, Chimney Swifts inhabit urban and residential areas with chimneys and buildings for nest sites and for group roosts.

Year-round	Summer
Migration	Winter

Grasslands, Edges and Cliff Habitat

Barn Swallow

Hirundo rustica

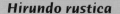

Length: 6–7½ inches (15–19 cm)
Wingspan: 11½–12½ inches (29 –32 cm)

male

The short, flattened and wide beak acts like an insect net to scoop up prey in flight

Steel blue above and rusty below with rusty forehead

Long forked tail with extra-long outer streamers

Juveniles look similar to adults but duller in color and less forked tail

Long, tapered wings

Long narrow toes for perching on branches, cliffs and wires

"Chirp-chatter" is called out between all swallows. "Whistle," call is given between a paired male and female.

En face. En l'air!

Choose a seat near an open field and settle in; the ballet is set to begin. En face. En l'air! With pirouettes, swoops and turns as acrobatic and graceful as a corps de ballet, Barn Swallows fly low over a field. They are in fact, eating on the wing by capturing flying prey in their wide, insect net of a bill. This dance of predator and prey is aided by their long narrow wings and forked tail that can be spread to brake or turn rapidly. Certain males are virtuosos. They have the longest tail streamers and the greatest tail and wing symmetry. This can be crucial during extreme weather conditions when flying insects are few. Virtuoso males are also chosen first by females as a mate.

Today's Special
Flies, beetles and moths

Habitat Café

Yumm . . . bring an order of flying insects. Barn Swallows are insectivores, eating a diet of entirely insects. They swoop and twist to catch insects in mid-air with their wide open mouth—called sweeping. When cold, wet weather lasts for days and insects are not flying, Barn Swallows can get very hungry. If it lasts for too long, it can be dangerous for swallows.

SPRING, SUMMER, FALL, WINTER MENU:
🪰 Flying insects

Life Cycle

NEST Barn Swallows nest in cliffs, caves, barns, bridges and culverts. Both parents build the nest cup of mud and grass stems just below a roof or ledge. Pebbles of mud are collected in their beak with as many as 1,400 mud pellets in a nest. First a narrow mud shelf is made and then built up on the sides. The shallow cup is lined with fine grass stems, hair or algae and then with wool or soft feathers.

EGGS About ¾ inch long. The clutch of 3–7 eggs is incubated by both parents for about 13–15 days.

MOM! DAD! Altricial. Parents keep the young warm by brooding them until their feathers grow in. Other adult Barn Swallows may help build the nest, incubate the eggs and brood the young.

NESTLING The parents catch flying insects and then compress them into a ball (bolus) in their throat. The nestling with their mouth closest to the parent and opened the widest gets the food pellet. In time, all are fed.

FLEDGLING The young leave the nest at about three weeks of age.

JUVENILE In late summer, juveniles gather with other swallows in migratory groups. They are mature enough on their spring return to nest.

Do the Math

Barn Swallows turn and swoop quickly on the wing, but their flight is relatively slow so they can scan for prey in flight. This flight is powered by a large wing surface that supports their body weight, a ratio called wing loading. This ratio of body weight to wing area is different among species of birds. Is it generally true that the larger the bird, the heavier the wing load? To answer this loaded question, Do the Math (page 194) with ratios of some birds featured in this book.

When
Diurnal. Barn Swallows are active during the day and rest at night.

Migration
Spring Arrival: Apr–May
Fall Departure: Aug–Sep
Mid- to long-distance migrant. Barn Swallows migrate in flocks to wintering areas in Central and South America.

Nesting
Barn Swallows begin nest construction in May in the Northeastern US. Breeding habitat is often an open area near water. Swallows need mud for nest building.

Getting Around
Barn Swallows only take to the ground for nesting material, where they shuffle on their short legs. When perching, they sidle along a wire or branch. Their bursts of straight flight include sharp turns and dives. Aerodynamic lift and the ability to turn is created by their deeply forked tail and long outer tail-streamers.

Where to Look
In the Northeastern US, Barn Swallows can be seen skimming low over fields, often near water in agricultural areas, cities and suburbs and along highways.

| Year-round | Summer |
| Migration | Winter |

Grasslands, Edges and Cliff Habitat

Eastern Bluebird

Sialia sialis

Length: 6½–8½ inches (15–20 cm)
Wingspan: 10–12½ inches (25–32 cm)

Short, stout bill slightly notched at the tip for catching insects

Male is sky blue above

Rusty-orange throat and breast

White belly

female

Females are duller in color than males

Young look like females but are speckled, and have blue wings

"Tury, cherwee, cheye-ley."
Male loudly sings this song to claim his territory.
The same song is sung softly to tell the female on the nest, "Everything's O.K., dear."

Wildlife Hotel: Immediate Occupancy

Bluebirds need tree cavities for nesting. Some people view an aging tree as useless and cut it down. An older tree or a rotting tree is a wildlife hotel complete with buffet dining, single occupancy or condominiums. In the Northeastern US, folks teamed up and built bluebird nesting boxes and placed them along forest edges and open rural and suburban areas that bluebirds need for catching insects. As a result, the number of Eastern Bluebirds in the Northeast has increased. You can become a part of this success story by planting and leaving valuable habitat and building and monitoring your own bluebird nesting boxes. Learn more from the your state's Bluebird Society.

Today's Special
caterpillars

Habitat Café

Yumm . . . bring an order of crickets, beetles, grasshoppers, ants, spiders, earthworms, snails and berries. Eastern Bluebirds are omnivorous. Put wiggly mealworms on the ground to invite a blue visitor. Most pet shops have mealworms.

SPRING, SUMMER, FALL MENU:
🐜 Lots of insects, some fruits and berries

WINTER MENU:
🐜 More fruits and berries than summer, but insects are still the main course

Life Cycle

NEST The female builds the nest cup of grasses in a natural tree cavity made by other birds such as woodpeckers, or in the tops of rotten fence posts, or in nesting boxes.

EGGS About ¾ inch long. The female incubates the clutch of 4–5 eggs for 12–14 days.

MOM! DAD! Altricial. The parents feed their young right after the chicks are born until three weeks after they leave the nest.

NESTLING The gray, downy chicks will begin to look like a female or male at about 1½ weeks of age. By then, their feathers have grown in and they leave the nest.

FLEDGLING If you hear *Tu-a-wee*, near a nesting cavity or box you will know that a young bluebird is leaving the nest to perch on a nearby limb or in cover. They also give this call when they are waiting for their parents to feed them.

JUVENILE In one year, they are mature enough to nest.

Unsolved Mystery

Is global warming affecting the seasonal movement of birds that nest in the Northeastern US? Are they returning earlier, leaving later or not leaving at all? Solving this mystery requires clues (records) from people all over the Northeast. In recent years individuals that have kept journals with bluebird departure and return dates have noted some changes. Keep your records in the journal section, pages 188–189. Be a part of solving this global mystery!

When
Eastern Bluebirds are diurnal. They feed during the day and rest at night.

Migration
Spring Arrival: Mar
Fall Departure: Sep–Nov
Short- to mid-distance migrant to the central and southeastern US and northern Mexico. Some may stay all year.

Nesting
Eastern Bluebirds begin nesting in the Northeastern US as early as March, more commonly in April. They may raise 1–3 broods per summer.

Getting Around
Eastern Bluebirds sidle—they move sideways. They hop and walk sideways while turning halfway around. How does it scratch its head? By moving a foot up and over a drooping wing. They are true-blue acrobats! Bluebirds fly low in open areas, about 10–12 feet above the ground. Their flight is higher on longer journeys.

Where to Look
Open habitats along deciduous forest edges.

Year-round   Summer
Migration   Winter

Brown-headed Cowbird

Molothrus ater

Length: 7½–9 inches (21–24 cm)
Wingspan: 9–12 inches (22–30 cm)

Short conical bill

Glossy black with brown head and neck

female

Female is smaller than male and has gray or brown plumage

Juveniles are streaked below

Fairly long pointed wings

"Glug glug glee." Males sing this song and if another cowbird is near, they bow.

Buffalo Birds

The buffalo that once roamed the open prairies were not alone. Brown-headed Cowbirds followed them, eating both insects they kicked up and insects living in their dung. Cowbirds didn't have time to stop and nest. Instead, they laid their eggs in the nests of birds that live where the prairie and forest meet. A female cowbird lays up to 40 eggs each year, none of which she hatches. Forest-edge nesters like Song Sparrows are recipients of cowbird eggs. Cowbirds do not reimburse the host species for incubation, meals and around the clock chick-care. Host species have adapted strategies in turn. They push the cowbird eggs out, build over the top, abandon the nest, or accept the eggs and raise the young.

Today's Special
egg shells

Habitat Café

Yumm . . . bring an order of grain and weed seeds with a side order of insects. Brown-headed Cowbirds are omnivorous, they eat both plant and animal matter. Buffalo and cattle allow cowbirds to hitch a ride while the birds eat the blood-sucking flies that feed on them.

SPRING, SUMMER, FALL, WINTER MENU:
Mostly seeds and crop grains with some insects

Life Cycle

NEST The female does not form a brood patch for incubating; rather, she lays her eggs in the nest of one or more of 144 host species. She locates a nest by watching for the host female to leave her nest. Laying eggs in multiple nests increases the cowbird's success by spreading out the risks.

EGGS About ¾ to 1 inch long. The eggs hatch after about 11–12 days, often before the eggs of the host species.

MOM! DAD! Altricial. The chicks hatch completely dependent on their host parents for food and warmth. They are usually larger than the host bird chicks.

NESTLING One way to survive is to be the biggest, loudest beak in the nest. As a result, cowbird chicks grow faster than the host species.

FLEDGLING The young leave the nest at 8–13 days after hatching. They stay nearby while the host parents feed them for another week or so.

JUVENILE The young join a large group with other cowbirds, black-birds, grackles and starlings to prepare for migration. They are mature enough the following spring to lay their eggs in another species' nest.

Do You Know?

To fool host parents, female cowbirds will remove an egg from the host nest before they lay their own egg inside. This behavior may limit the number of eggs in the host nest to a manageable level for the parents to incubate and feed. Most of the host species are not harmed by the arrangement as they have adapted over time to accommodate the loss to their own species. However, species that have very specific habitat and food requirements, such as the Kirkland's Warbler (found in Michigan) can be threatened by cowbird parasitism.

When

Diurnal. Brown-headed Cowbirds are active during the day and rest at night.

Migration

Spring Arrival: Mar–Apr
Fall Departure: Sep–Nov
Short-distance migrant to areas in the southeastern US. They travel about 500 miles between their spring and wintering areas. Flying at 30 miles per hour, how long does it take a flock to reach their destination? Do the math!

Nesting

Brown-headed Cowbirds begin laying their eggs in the nests of host species in May in the Northeastern US.

Getting Around

Cowbirds search for seeds and insects by walking and running on the ground. When singing, a male ruffles his back feathers, spreads his tail, lifts and spreads his wings and bows. He then wipes his bill. Males may perform this together—what a sight!

Where to Look

Cowbirds are found in many habitats. With forest fragmentation, their range has increased. Look for them in low trees of grasslands, fields and pastures, edge habitats and brushy thickets.
· *Super Adaptor*

| Year-round | Summer |
| Migration | Winter |

Grasslands, Edges and Cliff Habitat

127

Eastern Kingbird

Tyrannus tyrannus

Length: 7½–9 inches (22–31 cm)
Wingspan: 13–15 inches (33–38 cm)

Black head with hidden red "king's" crown; when excited, the male raises his head feathers to show off his crown

White chin

Gray on top with a white belly and underside

Males, females and juveniles look very much alike

Black tail with white band

"Chatter-zeer" could be "Hi. I'm back." Or a male telling others that he's patrolling his territory.

Tyrant of the Air

Tyrants are bullies. *Tyrannosaurus rex* dinosaurs are thought to have bullied other dinosaurs, earlier in earth's history. *Tyrannus tyrannus*, the Eastern Kingbird, is known today for bullying bigger birds to claim its territory and protect its young. If a hawk, crow, or owl flies even 100 feet above an Eastern Kingbird nest, watch out. The kingbird will mount a full aerial attack that includes chasing and crashing into the bigger bird from above while screeching *Zeeeer*! The predator is . . . out of there.

Today's Special
fresh wasps

Habitat Café

Yumm . . . bring an order of dragonflies, drone bumblebees, beetles and grasshoppers. Eastern Kingbirds are omnivorous. They feed on insects in the Northeast and fruits in their South American wintering grounds

SPRING, SUMMER, FALL MENU:
 Almost entirely insects, some berries

SUMMER MENU:
Mostly fruit, a few insects

Life Cycle

NEST The female builds the messy, but sturdy, nest 10–20 feet above the ground with plant stems and small twigs on a tree limb. She lines the nest with soft cottonwood or cattail down.

EGGS About 1 inch long. The female incubates the clutch of 3–4 eggs for 14–10 days.

MOM! DAD! Altricial. Both Mom and Dad help feed the young.

NESTLING The chicks hatch naked with orange skin and their eyes closed. After the first day, the colorful skin changes to gray and feathers begin to form.

FLEDGLING The young normally leave the nest when they are able to fly weakly, at about 2½ weeks. The parents kill prey, mostly flying insects, and remove the stingers from bees and wasps before feeding them to the young. Ouch! What parents will do for their kids!

JUVENILE Juveniles stay in the family group until just before fall migration. They are ready to date, mate and raise their own young when they return to the Northeast in the spring.

Did You Know?

Kingbirds wait on their perch for a flying insect to come near. They snatch it from the air in a short, quick flight called "hawking." How does a bird overcome gravity to fly? How does it fly against "drag," the resistance of the air flowing over its body in flight? Wing shape and physics. If you haven't studied flight yet, turn to page 192 for a wing-up on lift and Bernoulli's Principle, and learn about wing-loading on page 195.

When
Eastern Kingbirds are diurnal. They feed during the day and rest at night.

Migration
Spring Arrival: Late Apr–May
Fall Departure: Aug–Sep
Mid- to long-distance migrant. Migrate during the day in flocks of 10–60 birds to Central and South America, as far as Peru and Argentina.

Nesting
Eastern Kingbirds begin nesting in late May–June in the Northeastern US.

Getting Around
Perch on plants, fence posts or branches. The male does a "tumble flight." First, he flies high in a fluttering flight. Next, in short glides and aerobatic tumbles, he falls to the earth, Red Baron style. Good grief!

Where to Look
Most of the Northeastern US along roadsides, grasslands, fields and open areas near water. Look for Eastern Kingbirds perched on dead branches along lakes while you're fishing.

Grasslands, Edges and Cliff Habitat

Northern Bobwhite

Colinus virginianus

Length: 8–11 inches (20–28 cm)
Wingspan: 13 inches (33 cm)

female

Small, round, brown and white speckled body with short tail and neck

Female has buff-colored throat and eye stripe

Juvenile is similar to adult female but duller

Throat is white with black collar

Brown chest and white belly with dark feather edges

Males whistle their name. Listen for "Bobwhite!" to start low and end on a very high note.

A Covey of Quail

Birds that spend their time on the ground are in the company of alert predators: coyotes, fox, owls and hawks. Survival requires defense strategies that include camouflage, grouping up, and wings built for quick take off. An individual bobwhite will run for cover, freeze and then flush in instant flight when it is threatened. During fall and winter, bobwhites gather into family groups of 12 to 30 birds called a covey. During the night the covey roosts in a tight circle, each bird facing outward listening and watching for predators. For protection a covey will sit motionless, like a single camouflaged animal, but when a predator gets too close the entire covey quickly scatters to the air in different directions leaving a very confused predator.

Today's Special
Cracked and
shelled corn
BIRD FEEDER TREAT

Habitat Café

Yumm . . . bring an order of seeds and insects with a salad of fresh green leaves sprinkled with an occasional berry. They eat seeds from at least 650 different seed foods. Northern Bobwhite are omnivorous.

SPRING MENU:
🌱 Green leaves

SUMMER MENU:
Grass seeds and insects

FALL & WINTER MENU:
Wild plant and crop seeds

Life Cycle

NEST Both the female and male work together to chose the site and build the nest. They scrape a 1-foot-wide and 2-inch-deep depression in the ground and line it with dead grasses. The nest is hidden by an arched roof of plants.

EGGS About 1 inch long. It takes the female about 18 days to lay the clutch of 12–15 creamy white eggs. She usually incubates the eggs on her own for about 23 days, but Dad may pitch in. Northern Bobwhite chicks learn to recognize the call of their own parent while still in the egg!

MOM! DAD! Precocial. The chicks hatch with fluffy down and are ready to leave the nest. Parents lead the chicks to food on their first day. The chicks eat mostly insects during their first weeks gradually adding seeds and plants as they grow. Both Mom and Dad brood the chicks for the first two weeks.

JUVENILE The juveniles stay with their parents through most of the first winter, often in family groups called a covey. The young birds are mature enough to mate the following spring.

Did You Know?

The Northern Bobwhite is a game bird; it can be hunted during a specific law-enforced hunting season. The dates of the season and the number of birds that can be taken by a single hunter in a season are regulated by state and/or district agencies such as a Department of Natural Resources. Most states have a hunter education course that beginning hunters must successfully complete before gaining a license. Hunters must follow strict safety laws that protect both people and wildlife. Check out pages 196-197 for more information about your state or district.

When
Diurnal. Northern Bobwhites are active during the day and rest at night.

Migration
Permanent resident. They rarely travel more than half a mile from their breeding territories. Coveys may move around in a "fall shuffle" to spread themselves across habitat. Sounding like a round-up, they communicate movements to their group, "Hoy, hoy-poo, hoyee."

Nesting
Northern Bobwhites begin nesting in March–April with egg-laying in May in most of the Northeastern region.

Getting Around
Their flight from one place to another is low and short. When on the ground they walk and run quickly.

Where to Look
In the Northeastern US, Northern Bobwhites live in brushy fields, pastures, croplands, open pine and mixed pine-hardwood forests. Plant a small food plot of bush clover and stock a winter ground-feeding station with cracked corn.

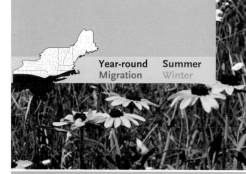

Year-round   Summer
Migration   Winter

Grasslands, Edges and Cliff Habitat

Eastern Meadowlark

Sturnella magna

Length: 7½–10 inches (19–26 cm)
Wingspan: 14–16 inches (35–40 cm)

in flight

Slender bill

Males are larger and
females are not as
brightly colored

Black "V" (bib)
on chest

Bright yellow
breast and belly

Short tail with
white edges
in flight

3-5 flute-like whistles
slurred together sliding
high to low,
"See you at school soon!"

Long legs
and toes

Woolly Mammoths and Meadowlarks

What do they have in common? Fossil records show that they both lived in North America over 10,000 years ago. Woolly Mammoths are extinct; there are no more Woolly Mammoths living on earth. Meadowlarks are still here, but with continued habitat loss, their numbers continue to fall. Male Eastern Meadowlarks use 7–8 acres of grassland for their breeding territory (space). What can you do? In rural locales, set aside a large grassy area free of chemicals and predators. Wait to mow, hay, or graze the area until after nesting season. Include a tall post for a meadowlark to stretch its bill to the sky and sing. Set up your spotting scope. Watch and listen for a new black-bibbed neighbor!

Habitat Café

Today's Special
crickets

Yumm . . . bring an order of crickets, grasshoppers and seeds with a side order of wild fruits. Eastern Meadowlarks are omnivorous and eat plant and animal matter. They probe for grubs and worms by "gaping" (putting their closed, pointed bill in the ground and opening it).

SPRING, SUMMER, FALL MENU:
Mostly insects, some seeds and fruit

WINTER MENU:
Weed seeds, field grains (corn) and some wild fruits

Life Cycle

NEST The female builds a dome-like nest in a grassy field. A deep spot in the ground is filled with large grasses and then lined with fine, soft grasses. A dome is built over the top by weaving together plants growing around the nest. An opening is left on one side of the nest with a path through the grass for coming and going.

EGGS About 1 inch long. The female incubates the 2–6 eggs for 13–14 days. If the nest is disturbed, the female will leave and not go back to incubate the eggs. Respect the need for safe nesting.

MOM! DAD! Altricial. Mom does most of the feeding. Dad does not go to the nest. He may catch insects and "beak" them over to Mom.

NESTLING Nestlings need to eat more than half of their body weight in food each day. Mom averages 100 trips per day to gather insects for her famished brood.

FLEDGLING With long, quick legs and the ability to hide in plants, the young leave the nest at about 1½ weeks of age. Their parents feed them for two more weeks, until they can fly.

JUVENILE They look like their parents but with spots instead of a black bib on their chest. In one year, they are mature enough to nest.

Did You Know?

Each meadowlark male has his own large (up to 80 or more) collection of songs. Meadowlarks learn songs during a specific period of time when they are young. If they do not hear the song of an Eastern Meadowlark during this window of learning, they will adopt a song from another bird species. Eastern Meadowlarks have even taken on the song of a Northern Cardinal!

When
Meadowlarks are diurnal. They feed during the day and rest at night.

Migration
Spring Arrival: Mar–Apr
Fall Departure: Oct
Short- to mid-distance migrant. Spends winter in areas with temperatures above 10 degrees, as far south as Mexico. In spring, males arrive 2–4 weeks ahead of females to set up territories.

Nesting
Eastern Meadowlarks begin nesting in April–May in the Northeastern US.

Getting Around
Meadowlarks walk and run on the ground. When a female meadowlark nears her nest, she walks closer to the ground to hide from predators. Their flight is a glide followed by quick wingbeats. They can fly 20–40 miles per hour.

Where to Look
Open grasslands and uncropped fields, salt marshes, hayfields, pastures and grassy roadsides.

Year-round   Summer
Migration   Winter

Grasslands, Edges
and Cliff Habitat

133

Killdeer

Charadrius vociferus

Length: 8–11 inches (20–28 cm)
Wingspan: 18–19 inches (46–48 cm)

injury-feigning display

Olive-brown

Rusty orange rump patch is seen when tail is spread

Both the male and the female have two black bands across their breast

White underside

Long legs for wading in the shallow water and running fast

"Kill—deer, kill—deer!" or, "Sound the alarm! Danger near!"

Best Drama Award

The Killdeer spread out and crushed on the ground in front of you looks like a dying bird uttering its last painful *dee*. As if trying to avoid a certain death, the Killdeer limps along with a broken wing. Watch it long enough and the wing may suddenly heal. Poor bird? Smart, tricky bird that has just lured a predator away from its young by pretending to be injured. This behavior is called an "injury-feigning display." The Killdeer fakes an injury to protect its young. Your part in this drama is that of a responsible neighbor. Watch the nesting area from afar with a spotting scope or binoculars. Your reward will be more Killdeer to watch in the future. Take a bow.

Today's Special
crayfish

Habitat Café

Yumm . . . bring an order of grasshoppers, beetles, earthworms, ticks, and mosquito larvae with a side of green tree frog. Killdeer are omnivorous.

SPRING, SUMMER, FALL MENU:
Mostly insects, crustaceans and amphibians, some seeds

WINTER MENU:
Entirely insects and crustaceans

When
Killdeer are diurnal. They feed during the day and rest at night. Migrate by day and night.

Migration
Spring Arrival: Late Feb–Mar
Fall Departure: Sep–Nov
Mid- to long-distance migrant. Killdeer migrate south in flocks of up to 30 birds to Central and South America. They are one of the first spring arrivals to the Northeastern US.

Nesting
Killdeer nest in the Northeastern US beginning as early as March.

Life Cycle

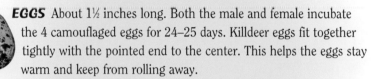

NEST The nest is a simple, low scrape in the ground. It is lined with pebbles, gravel, or wood chips that help keep the eggs from rolling away with wind and rain. They will also nest on flat rooftops and in gravel parking lots.

EGGS About 1½ inches long. Both the male and female incubate the 4 camouflaged eggs for 24–25 days. Killdeer eggs fit together tightly with the pointed end to the center. This helps the eggs stay warm and keep from rolling away.

MOM! DAD! Precocial. Parents do not feed the chicks. As soon as the chicks have hatched and their down is dry, the parents lead them to feeding areas. Parents brood the young for the first few days and guard them for the first ten days. Chicks can swim across small streams.

FLEDGLING If a predator comes near, chicks lay low and freeze. Some will raise their legs above the grass to look like a stem or stick. Killdeer stay with their parents and siblings until they can fly at 3–4 weeks of age.

JUVENILE Killdeer can nest and mate when they are one year of age. Juveniles have one black neck band.

Getting Around
Killdeer have a standard ground move: run a short ways, stop, bob their head and run again. They keep their body straight while their long legs are a blur of motion. In flight, they are strong and fast at speeds of 28–35 miles per hour. Adult Killdeer can swim in fast-flowing water.

Where to Look
Originally a shorebird found on mud flats and sandbars, the Killdeer has adapted to open habitats: fields, grazed pastures, golf courses, gravel parking lots, flat rooftops, soccer fields, airports and playgrounds.
· *Super Adaptor*

Did You Know?

Nesting on a rooftop can be dangerous. Killdeer in this situation can be creative when it is time to lead their newly hatched chicks to food. One pair of Killdeer parents called to their chicks from the ground near the base of a rain gutter. The chicks heard the parents call to come down from the roof and they used the rainspout as a slide.

| Year-round | Summer |
| Migration | Winter |

American Kestrel

Falco sparverius

Length: 9–12 inches (22–31 cm)
Wingspan: 20–24 inches (51–61 cm)

Black-and-white face pattern

Hooked, sharp beak

Narrow body, long tail

Markings on the back of the head look like a pair of false eyes or "ocelli"

female

Females have red-brown wings and seven to nine dark bands across the tail and a brown-streaked breast; females are larger than males

Juveniles look like adults with dull colors

"Killy, killy, killy" means "Stay away!"

Build It and They Will Come

Build a kestrel nest box and place it on a tree or a pole near a grassy area with small mammals, insects and a few snakes for good measure, and these small falcons may come. In the Northeastern US, both kestrel nesting boxes and trees with hollow cavities found along the edges of open areas provide important structures for kestrels. Be involved. Build a nest box for kestrels. Ask your Audubon club for the best place to hang a nest box. Include a hinged lid to carefully check the inside of the box during nesting season and keep a record of the number of eggs, young and adults. Make an older tree in your yard a wildlife tree and watch these handy neighbors as they eat unwelcome insects and rodents!

Today's Special

ground squirrels

Habitat Café

Yumm . . . bring an order of mice, snakes, lizards, caterpillars, beetles, dragonflies, crickets and a few small birds and animals. American Kestrels are carnivorous. Kestrel parents plan for the kids' extra snacks and poor weather conditions by caching prey.

SPRING, SUMMER, FALL MENU:
Mostly insects, some birds and animals

WINTER MENU:
All small animals

Life Cycle

NEST Kestrels prefer to nest in a woodpecker hole or natural tree cavity at the edge of a wooded area. With the loss of nesting habitat, they have adapted to using nest boxes near their food. They do not bring in nesting materials but may add feathers. A few wood chips may be placed in the bottom of a nest box.

EGGS About 1½ inches long. The female incubates the 4–5 eggs for 30 days. The male takes over when the female leaves for a short time each day. Both have a "brood patch," an area on the belly without feathers. Putting a bare belly to eggs keeps them warm.

MOM! DAD! Altricial. Both Mom and Dad help feed the young.

NESTLING The brown-gray chicks stay in the nest for 30 days.

FLEDGLING Parents feed the young for the first two weeks after they leave the nest.

JUVENILE The first year is the hardest for birds to survive. According to research, only 4 out of 10 kestrels reach their first birthday.

Gross Factor

How do some bird species determine the most productive hunting areas? They see the urine trails left by their prey. The urine of voles and other small mammals contains nitrogen components (chemical parts) that reflect ultraviolet (UV) light. Many birds, but not people, can see UV light and can detect the small mammal runways marked by urine along the ground!

When
American Kestrels are diurnal. They feed during the day and rest at night.

Migration
Spring Arrival: Apr
Fall Departure: Sep–Oct
Short- to mid-distance migrant. Some kestrels stay year-round in the Northeastern US or until snow covers the ground and prey is hard to find. Some migrate as far south as Mexico and Panama.

Nesting
American Kestrels nest in April in the Northeastern US.

Getting Around
Kestrels hover in one place by facing into the wind with their wings spread. Their boomerang-shaped wings have a notch in the outer three primary feathers to aid in hovering. The tail is used as a rudder to steady the bird while it searches for prey below. Kestrels perch on utility lines and poles and look for prey.

Where to Look
American Kestrels hunt for prey along rural and urban roadways, pastures and open fields and grassy railroad right-of-ways with access to a natural perch, nesting tree, or nest box.

Year-round	Summer
Migration	Winter

Peregrine Falcon

Falco peregrinus

Length: 14–19 inches (36–49 cm)
Wingspan: 39½–43 inches (100–110 cm)

soaring

Black head with dark cheek patch or "moustache" below eye

Hooked bill with a notch on the cutting edge, called a tomial tooth, for tearing apart flesh

Blue-gray above

Females are larger and heavier than males; juveniles have a pale crown

Light underneath with dark spots and horizontal bars

Pointed, angular wings and short tail

"Kak kak kak kak." Both the male and female use this call when there is a threat to them or to their territory.

The World's Fastest Animal

The world's fastest animal took a population dive in the 1950s. By 1964, Peregrine Falcons were gone as a breeding species in the eastern US. Chemical pesticides, including DDT, had traveled through the food chain and into the bird's eggshells making them too thin to incubate. In 1970, peregrines were given protection as a federally endangered species and soon the use of DDT was banned in the US. With the teamwork of The Peregrine Fund, National Audubon Society, federal and state agencies and volunteers, young captive-reared peregrines were released at potential nesting sites. By 1999 the Peregrine Falcon was unlisted as federally threatened, although it remains listed as endangered in some states.

Habitat Café

Yumm . . . bring an order of small- to medium-sized birds (from a menu of over 400 species) with a side order of bats and other small mammals. Peregrine Falcons are carnivorous, they eat only animal matter. City-dwelling peregrines feed on pigeons and starlings while peregrines nesting near water feed on shorebirds and ducks.

SPRING, SUMMER, FALL, WINTER MENU:
🐦 Small- to medium-sized birds

Life Cycle

NEST Peregrines nest on ledges 50–200 feet above ground on rock cliffs or on tall buildings, bridges, or nesting towers, often near a river or lake. They lie forward and push their feet back to make a nest of a shallow scrape of small rocks, sand, or dirt.

EGGS About 2 inches long. The clutch of 3–5 eggs is incubated by the parents for about 33–35 days.

MOM! DAD! Semi-altricial. Covered with down, the chicks double their body mass in the first week.

NESTLING Parents feed the new hatchlings only muscle. After 2-3 weeks, the young are fed the entire carcass. Please pass the bones.

FLEDGLING At 40 days of age they stand on the ledge of the eyrie (nest), flap their wings and fly. For the first few weeks they follow Mom and Dad for food. Parents drop live prey for the young to capture and kill. City-dwelling peregrines learn to maneuver around tall buildings, vehicles and bridges.

JUVENILE At three years of age they can nest and raise their own young. Transmitters are attached to some peregrines to track their movements and learn even more about this speedy bird.

Birding Tip

Peregrines will need to be closely monitored for years to come; they had a close call. You can be a part of their future by educating others and supporting the private and public groups that work to monitor their progress. Remind your parents about the nongame wildlife check-off on their state tax returns. The donations benefit Peregrine Falcons and many other wildlife species. When you see a Peregrine Falcon it is a wild reminder of how important teamwork is to the future of the global environment.

When

Diurnal. Peregrine Falcons are active during the day and rest at night.

Migration

Spring Arrival: Mar–Apr
Fall Departure: Sep–Oct
Mid- to long-distance migrant traveling along the US East Coast and south to wintering areas in Central and South America. Some remain in their territory year-round.

Nesting

Peregrine Falcons begin nest construction in late March–April in the Northeastern US.

Getting Around

The Peregrine Falcon is capable of flying at speeds of 200 mph! To capture prey they go into a stoop (wings tight against their body in a free-fall dive), plunging downward with speed that often kills their prey on impact.

Where to Look

In the Northeastern US, Peregrine Falcons are found along cliffs near seacoasts, rivers and lakes, and in urban areas with tall buildings and bridges along large rivers.

Year-round	Summer
Migration	Winter

Grasslands, Edges and Cliff Habitat

Northern Harrier

Circus cyaneus

Length: 18–20 inches (46–50 cm)
Wingspan: 40–46½ inches (102–118 cm)

wheeling

White rump patch

Males are silver-gray above and lighter below

female

The females are brown above and cream and brown streaked below, with a banded tail

Juveniles look similar to females but are darker brown above and russet below

Black wingtips

"Kek, kek, kek" means "Stay away!"

Long, square tail

Flying Food Pass

Watch Northern Harriers during the summer. Watch closely. You may see the male perform a flying food pass. When he has a juicy mouse, he signals to the female on the nest below, "purrduk." She flies just under him, turns over and catches the mouse in her talons. A speedy delivery is made to the hungry chicks. Keep watch for Northern Harriers to pick up a mouse nest, shake it, then drop the nest. A litter of young mice and their parents are snatched up for a quick snack. How do they know the nest is full of mice? As they glide over grassy fields and prairies, harriers hear prey before they see. Their hearing is aided by a facial disk that funnels sound to their enlarged ear openings.

Today's Special
gophers

Habitat Café

Yumm . . . Bring an order of mice, voles, shrews, frogs, lizards and small perching birds. Northern Harriers are carnivorous. They eat only animal matter. When their main prey, meadow voles, increase in great numbers in a given year, the number of young harriers produced increases. Supply-side food economics!

SPRING, SUMMER, FALL, WINTER MENU:

Entirely animal matter

Life Cycle

NEST The female builds a pile of grass and weeds on the ground, hollowed in the top with a few sticks or twigs as the base.

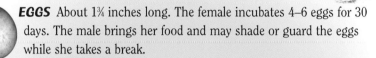

EGGS About 1¾ inches long. The female incubates 4–6 eggs for 30 days. The male brings her food and may shade or guard the eggs while she takes a break.

MOM! DAD! Altricial. Dad brings the food to Mom. She feeds the chicks by tearing the food into pieces as they take it from her bill. Unlike their quiet parents, the chicks use noisy screech calls to scare predators.

NESTLING When a chick strays from the nest, Mom carries it back home in her bill by the nape (back of neck). After two weeks of age, the young take paths through the grass to raised feeding and resting areas.

FLEDGLING As heavy as an adult, they can fly at one month of age and their meals come in an aerial pass from their parents. To practice capturing prey, the young pounce on objects on the ground.

JUVENILE Juveniles join with others their age, feeding and preparing for migration. It takes 2–3 years to gain their adult plumage and be mature enough to raise their own young.

Birding Tip

LOOK OUT OVERHEAD! These strong birds of prey will dive at and possibly even sink their talons into anyone that gets close to the nest. It's a good idea not to disturb the nest or nesting area during this sensitive time. Adults may abandon the young and you may be in danger. Safety first, for everyone!

When

Northern Harriers are diurnal. They can spend 40 percent of their day in flight, logging up to 100 miles per day!

Migration

Spring Arrival: March-Apr
Fall Departure: late Aug–Nov
Mid-distance migrant. Flying alone, they migrate to Texas, Mexico, Costa Rica and Panama. A few may overwinter in the Northeast.

Nesting

Northern Harriers begin nesting in April–May in the Northeastern US.

Getting Around

Look for Northern Harriers in an open field flying low (10–13 feet) over the ground with their slim, lightweight body, and long wings. They fly with a series of flaps and tilting glides, their wings held in a spread-out "V." Their outer 3-5 primary flight feathers are notched for aerodynamic soaring.

Where to Look

Undisturbed grasslands, wet meadows, inland and coastal marshes in the Northeastern US.

Year-round   Summer
Migration   Winter

Grasslands, Edges and Cliff Habitat   141

Red-tailed Hawk

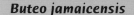
Buteo jamaicensis

Length: 18–25 inches (46–63 cm)
Wingspan: 4–5 feet (122–152 cm)

soaring

Dark head and upper side, lighter underside

White underside with brown streaks on belly that may resemble a band

Male and female look the same, but the female is larger, stronger

"Kee-eee-arr!" or, "This is my territory."

Tail is "red" on upper side with a narrow, dark band

Only adult hawks have red tails

Migration Skyways

Tens of thousands of birds move along the migratory skyway over the Atlantic coastline and inland mountain ridges from September–November and again March–May. From Cape May, Hawk Mountain, Acadia National Park, Little Round Top, Braddock Bay and more lookouts you can view Red-tailed Hawks and other raptors, as well as shorebirds, waterfowl and songbirds on the move. You don't have to wait until migration to see Red-tailed Hawks. Their rust-colored tails flash overhead from spring through fall (some all year) and they have become more common along rural and urban roadways. Look for red-tails perched on power lines, in trees, and on billboards scanning roadside ditches for a meal of rabbit and rodents.

142

Today's Special
muskrats

Habitat Café

Yumm . . . bring an order of rabbits, mice, voles, chipmunks, squirrels, snakes, gophers, skinks and pheasants. Red-tailed Hawks are carnivorous. Sharp, hooked beak and talons are used for capturing and tearing apart prey. Taken to a feeding perch, small mammals are swallowed whole and birds are beheaded, plucked and eaten. Bill-licking good.

SPRING, SUMMER, FALL, WINTER MENU:
 Mostly mammals, some reptiles, birds and amphibians

Life Cycle

NEST The male and female build the bulky nest in a large tree, 30–90 feet from the ground. They may return to the same nest for several years, adding more sticks and lining it with moss, evergreen twigs and grapevine bark. Nests that are reused for years can be over three feet deep!

EGGS Slightly more than 2¼ inches long. The female and male incubate the 2–3, dull, creamy white eggs for 28–35 days.

MOM! DAD! Altricial. Both Mom and Dad feed the young. At first the parents tear off pieces of prey for the chicks, but as they grow, the parents leave the food for the young to tear apart on their own. Learning to be independent is a big deal in the bird world!

NESTLING Fluffy down begins to be replaced by new feathers when the chicks are about two weeks of age.

FLEDGLING Young Red-tailed Hawks leave the nest and fly when they are 6–7 weeks old.

JUVENILE Immature hawks have a gray-brown tail with dark bands. It takes two years to develop the red tail. Immature Red-tailed Hawks begin to migrate south before the adults in the fall.

Unsolved Mystery

Several species of hawks regularly place a fresh, leafy branch(es) in the nest with the chicks every day. Why? To shade the young? To hide the young from predators? Do the aromatic oils in the leaves help control parasites on the chicks' skin? To solve this mystery use a spotting scope from far away. Parent hawks will not go near the nest if they suspect it is being watched.

When

Red-tailed Hawks are diurnal, feeding during the day and resting at night.

Migration

Spring Arrival: Mar–May
Fall departure: Sep–Dec
Permanent resident to short-distance migrant to the southern US and Mexico. Some over-winter in the Northeastern US near fields and along roadsides including interstate highways.

Nesting

Red-tailed Hawks begin egg laying in March–May in the Northeastern US.

Getting Around

Red-tailed Hawks soar, perch and fly low to the ground to find prey with their keen eyesight. Once they spot it, they dive or pounce on their prey, carrying it away in their strong talons. Look high in the sky for a soaring Red-tailed Hawk with its tail and wings spread out, seemingly motionless.

Where to Look

Red-tailed Hawks prefer open areas with large trees nearby for perching but also hunt for prey along both rural and urban roadsides throughout the Northeastern US.
· *Super Adaptor*

Year-round | Summer
Migration | Winter

Snowy Owl

Bubo scandiacus

Length: 21–26 inches (53–66 cm)
Wingspan: 4–5 feet (122–152 cm)

female

Females have heavy brown-gray bars across their wings and body

Large, yellow eyes

Blue-black, hooked bill

Males are pure white with a few dark spots on their body and wings

Long, broad wings

Immature owls are more heavily marked than females

Feathered "insulated boots" keep the legs and feet warm; shiny black talons

The Ghosts of Winter

Winter ghosts come to the Northeast on snow-white wings. They come from the arctic tundra (open, flat arctic plains) of Canada in search of food. In years with a bumper crop of lemmings to eat in Canada, Snowy Owls raise a large clutch of young owls and do not migrate south. In years when food is scarce, they raise fewer young and move south for the winter. The Northeastern US does not have tundra, but watch in an open area for this owl, which can be mistaken for a large chunk of snow—look closer for the yellow eyes. Mind your wildlife watching manners and ask before entering private property.

Today's Special
voles

Habitat Café

Yumm . . . bring an order of lemmings, rabbits, snowshoe hares, fish and carrion (dead animal meat). Snowy Owls are carnivorous. Depending on their food supply, owls' lives can be feast or famine. When hunting is good, they can eat 1,600 lemmings in a single year; when times are tough, they can go long periods without food.

SPRING, SUMMER, FALL, WINTER MENU:
 Lemmings, voles, rabbits, fish, carrion

Life Cycle

NEST The female scrapes out a nest in the frozen turf and moss in an open, windswept site. If the nesting area becomes drifted with snow, she may abandon the nest and eggs.

EGGS About 2¼ inches long. The female incubates the clutch of 3–7 eggs for 30–33 days. In years when prey is plentiful she may lay up to 11 eggs.

MOM! DAD! Semi-altricial. The chicks have a gray down that absorbs the heat of the sun and camouflages them from predators. They open their eyes on the fifth day. Dad brings dinner and Mom picks out the soft heart and liver to feed the chicks.

NESTLING The young are able to walk from the nest at two weeks of age but do not leave the nest for another couple weeks.

FLEDGLING Dad brings whole prey to the young once they are out of their nest. By the time the owlets are on their own, they have eaten over 1,500 lemmings! They can fly well at seven weeks of age.

JUVENILE It takes 2–5 years for the young to be mature enough to date, mate, nest and raise their own young.

History Hangout

Birds have been a part of the culture of the Northeastern US throughout history. They provided a valuable source of food year-round. Parts of birds were used for making simple tools and their feathers provided warmth as well as utility. Pottery, clothing and tools were adorned with designs inspired by their natural form and behaviors. Cultural and prehistoric and historic areas are remarkable places to visit. While you are there be respectful of the significance of sacred areas to others.

When

Diurnal. They feed during the day and rest at night.

Migration

Fall arrival: Oct-Nov
Spring Departure: Mar-Apr
Boreal migrants that move into the northeastern US, when their food supply is scarce in Canada during the winter.

Nesting

Snowy Owls do not nest in the United States but move here from Canada for the winter when food is in short supply.

Getting Around

They perch in a spot where they can see all around and wait patiently for hours, listening for voles and lemmings under the snow. They swoop down over their prey and gulp—they eat small prey headfirst and whole.

Where to Look

Search open areas, on river ice and near the shores of the Great Lakes and the Atlantic Ocean coastline.

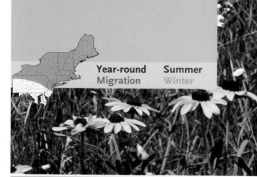

Year-round	Summer
Migration	Winter

Grasslands, Edges and Cliff Habitat

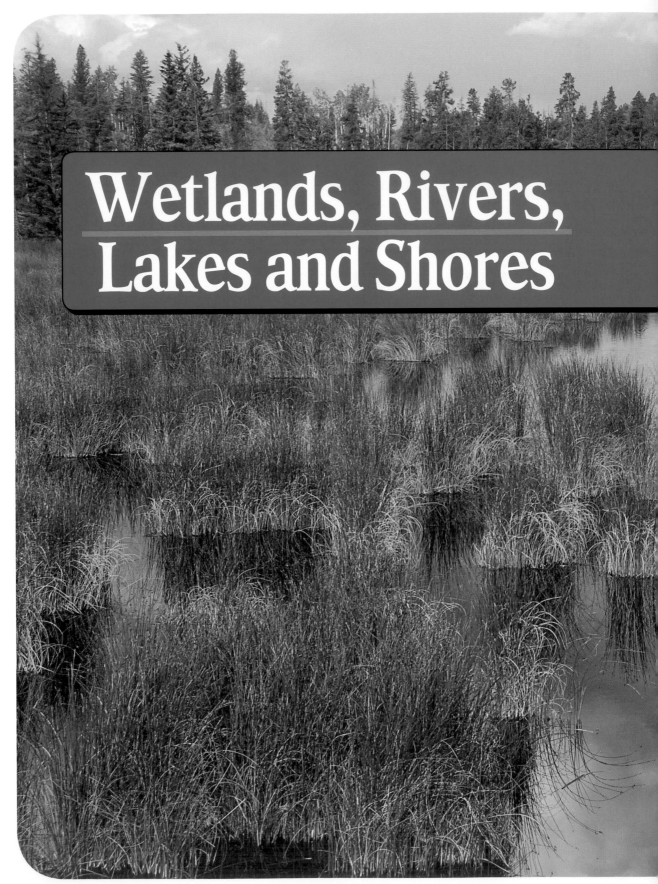

Wetlands, Rivers, Lakes and Shores

Water, water, everywhere! The Northeastern US has an abundance of wet habitats for birds. Bordered to the northwest by Lake Erie and Lake Ontario and to the east by the Atlantic Ocean, the region is also host to interior lakes, bogs, thousands of miles of rivers and streams, inland and coastal marshes, estuaries, bays and both freshwater and marine shores.

147

Why Does The Northeast Have So Much Water? Ice!

We can thank two million years of glacial action for many of the water areas in the Northeast. The last in the line of glaciations from the massive Laurentide Ice Sheet in Canada moved into the Northeastern US some 35,000–10,000 years ago. During growth spurts, it sent lobes of ice deep into the Northeast. The giant glacier spun its magic over the Northeast, altering the landscape and leaving icy glacial melt water that formed rivers and wetlands.

Bald Eagle

Its watery remains filled sunken areas as well, producing lakes and leaving its mark where the land meets the Atlantic Ocean. Today, the Great Lakes and Atlantic coastline are important to people and birds alike. They provide birds with major migration flyways. Visit the major rivers, Chesapeake and Delaware Bays and the shores of the Great Lakes and Atlantic coast for close-up views of migrating birds.

Wade Into Wetlands and Cruise the Coastline

Pull on your boots and take a pal to a wetland, bog, river, lake, or shore. Freshwater areas are great places to find tadpoles, giant water bugs, dragonflies, crayfish, beavers, river otters and birds. Along the Atlantic Coast you may find snails and crustaceans like barnacles, fiddler crabs and beach hoppers. Look for the unexpected, rare animals, too. Nearly half of threatened or endangered species live in or depend on water habitats.

Wetland habitats are important for other reasons, too. They help filter pollutants from run-off; help recharge groundwater supplies; and reduce flooding, by slowing the flow of rainwater on its way to streams and rivers. Water habitats are also super places to have fun. People canoe, kayak, hunt, fish, scout for seashells and enjoy nature. To ensure that they remain, public and private conservation and sporting groups and private citizens are working hard for their protection.

Great Egret

Water habitats come in many shapes, types and sizes. We talk about peat bogs in the coniferous habitat section (page 27). Other habitats include shorelines and beaches, inland and coastal marshes, wooded swamps and river floodplains, bays and estuaries. Each kind of water habitat has a special place in the Northeast's ecosystems.

Wood Duck

Where Do Water Birds Live?

Just as forests have different levels that support different species of birds, a shore, lake, wetland, or river has different areas, or zones, that support various plants and animals that birds in turn use for shelter and food.

Perched on an overhanging branch, the Belted Kingfisher scans the clear, shallow water for small fish to spear while busy Marsh Wrens flit among the cattails and reeds. With legs nearly as tall as the marsh grasses they wade through, Great Blue Herons silently stalk small fish, crayfish, frogs and giant water beetles.

Belted Kingfisher

Dabbling in the shallow waters with tails tipped skyward are colorful waterfowl—Mallards. Watching from a throne high in a waterside tree is the Osprey, ready to dive feet first and talons outstretched for a fish.

Other water birds, such as Pied-billed Grebes, are diving for fish like mini submarines. In the deep, clear waters of inland lakes during the summer and coastal waters in the winter, the black-and-white checkered Common Loon dives like a torpedo for fish. Along the shore of coastal waters American Oystercatchers chisel open mussels and oysters and the rare Piping Plover chicks scoot back and forth on the shore.

Some species, such as the Red-winged Blackbird, have adapted to living along roadways where there are cattails to perch on and insects to eat. Wildlife is everywhere!

Check Off the Wetlands Birds You See!

When you spot wetland birds, use these pages to check them off. The locations of these illustrations indicate where you might see them (air, water, edge, or shore).

Common Yellowthroat

Geothlypis trichas

Length: 4–5 inches (11–13 cm)
Wingspan: 6–7½ inches (15–19 cm)

Black mask with white upper band

Males have an olive-green back, wings and tail

Bright yellow throat and upper chest

Females do not wear a black mask and are more dull than males

Immature yellowthroats resemble an adult female

"Where-is-it, Where-is-it." Males sing this song to say this is where my territory is. Then, if you are too close for comfort they call out, "Tchat!"

Masked Super Bird of the Wetlands

"Faster than a speeding bullet, able to leap tall buildings in a single bound"—probably not, but this black-masked super bird can down over 80 aphids in a mere minute! Nearly always on the move, Common Yellowthroats dodge detection in the Northeast's damp areas of cattails, shrubs and grasses. You won't need x-ray vision to find them, just follow the sound and visual clues. Warblers warble— their song has a rhythmic move to it. Yellowthroats are warblers built for maneuvering through tight spaces. They glean insects in low plants with their short, thin bill. The latest marsh buzz? Clark Kent has something in common with this tiny super hero, but keep it under cover.

Today's Special
leafhoppers

Habitat Café

Yumm... bring an order of small insects with side orders of spiders and caterpillars. Common Yellowthroats are insectivores. A friend to plants, these warblers chow on leaf-eating insects. But watch out. Bigger birds like Northern Shrikes will make a meal of Common Yellowthroats!

SPRING, SUMMER, FALL, WINTER MENU:

 Mostly insects and spiders with a few seeds

Life Cycle

NEST The female builds the loose nest cup on or near the marshy ground where it is hidden from predators and shaded from the sun. The soft inner lining is made with finer grass.

EGGS About ½ to ¾ inch long. The female incubates the clutch of 3–5 eggs for 12 days.

MOM! DAD! Altricial. The orange-skinned, naked chicks are about 1 inch long and weigh less than a penny when they hatch—and that includes their black egg tooth.

NESTLING "Chac-chac-chac" coming from the nest means the chicks are begging for more food. Mom and Dad take different routes to and from the nest to deter any lurking predators.

FLEDGLING At only 10-12 days of age, the young leave the nest. Mom and Dad chip in groceries for a couple more weeks and then the juveniles are on their own.

JUVENILE By fall, young males begin to practice their beginning song before the family heads out on migration.

Birding Tip

Get a close-up view of birds by using binoculars. (A pair with a large field of vision, 8 x 40 plus, works well.) First spot the bird without binoculars. Then, keep your eyes on the bird while you lift the binoculars to your eyes. Think of the binoculars as now being attached like a pair of eyeglasses and move them directly with your head. With practice you will be able to zoom in on quick-winged warblers! Tip: Spotting scopes in public wildlife viewing areas are free to use during your visits.

When

Diurnal. Common Yellowthroats are active during the day and rest at night.

Migration

Spring Arrival: Apr–May
Fall Departure: Aug –Sep
Short- to mid-distance migrant by night to wintering areas located along the Gulf and Atlantic Coasts of the southeastern United States and northeastern Mexico.

Nesting

Common Yellowthroats begin nesting in the Northeastern US in May–June.

Getting Around

Common Yellowthroats hop and climb through thickets, grasses and sedges for spiders, insects and caterpillars. Their flight is flitting, short and direct. Flight song: Males fly up with their tail bobbing and wings quivering to each note in their song. They come back down silently to land near their starting point.

Where to Look

Cattail, coastal and inland marshes, thickets, bogs, river edges, damp fields and shrub areas over all of the Northeastern US.

| Year-round | Summer |
| Migration | Winter |

Marsh Wren

Cistothorus palustris

Length: 4–5½ inches (10–14 cm)
Wingspan: 6–7 inches (16–18 cm)

Dull black crown

White eyebrow line

Tail has small
black bands

Brown above,
black-and-white
streaked triangle
on upper back

Females and males look
similar but the male is
larger than the female

Long, slender
and slightly
curved bill to
probe for insects

White underside

Males sing a song that can
sound like many things,
including mud bubbles
popping underfoot.

Secret Agent Work Available

Zooming around the marsh cattails like plump, brown dragonflies, these tiny birds are, come a little closer, *secretive*. Wrens operate in disguise, camouflaged. Like their woodland cousins the House Wrens, Marsh Wren males build 2–10 houses. Why build so many round basket nests among marsh cattail and reed stalks of the Northeast's wet areas? It might be for decoy nests to fake out predators, or apartments for young birds when they leave the parents' nest. Or could it be to show off to the gals they are the big guy in the marsh? Solving the mystery of this crafty bird calls for a secret agent like you. Are those sunglasses with a detective camera in the rim? I hope they have a zoooom lens!

Habitat Café

Today's Special
spiders

Yumm... bring an order of bees, wasps, ants, leafhoppers, moths, beetles and bugs. Marsh Wrens are insectivores. Scientists have watched captive Marsh Wrens dip dry food in water and soften mealworms by beating them against a perch. Do Marsh Wrens do the same in the wild? Watch closely.

SPRING, SUMMER, FALL, WINTER MENU:
🐜 All Insects

Life Cycle

NEST The female weaves wet cattail and reed leaves into a dome-shaped nest basket attached to plant stalks, 1–3 feet above water. The nest is lined with cattail down, feathers and rootlets. How do they go in and out? A hole is left in the side of the nest basket.

EGGS About ½ to ¾ inch long. The female incubates the clutch of 4–6 eggs for 11–13 days.

MOM! DAD! Altricial. Hatched blind and helpless, chicks depend on Mom to feed them small insects and keep the nest clean. Dad is busy building nests and singing in a new area to attract another female. If he does come to the nest, Mom may chase him away. Marsh Wrens will destroy the eggs of their own kind and other species.

NESTLING As the chicks grow in size, so does the size of the insects they are fed. Mom is back and forth hunting and delivering dinner.

FLEDGLING Like little brown mice, the young leave the nest at about two weeks of age to move along the ground and hunt for food. Male chicks begin learning Dad's song at about the same time.

JUVENILE Juveniles group together for migration. On their spring return they are mature enough to date, mate and raise their own young.

Did You Know?

Male Marsh Wrens sing from 40 or more song patterns, sometimes even singing into the night. Why? With males competing for females, it's about setting up their home territory and getting a female to come over. When a female hears a male sing, it triggers body chemicals (hormones) that tell her body it is egg-laying time. To do this she first needs a mate—the male with the finest song in the marsh!

When

Marsh Wrens are diurnal. They are active during the day and rest at night. Males may sing into the night, serenading Marsh Wren females and evening visitors like you!

Migration

Spring Arrival: Apr–May
Fall Departure: Sep–Oct
Short- to mid-distance migrant by night to the southern United States Atlantic and Gulf Coasts. Some may overwinter along coastal marshes.

Nesting

Marsh Wrens begin nesting in May in the Northeastern US.

Getting Around

Marsh Wrens move in short flights with rapid wingbeats. Like acrobats on a high wire, they climb up and down cattail and reed stalks. They creep and hop along the ground, winding their way through the plants.

Where to Look

Marshes and wetlands with cattails throughout the Northeastern US.

Year-round	Summer
Migration	Winter

Spotted Sandpiper

Actitis macularius

Length: 7–8 inches (18–20 cm)
Wingspan: 14½–16 inches (37–40 cm)

winter

Females and males
look the same

White eye-ring

Black line from bill
across eye

Brown back

Long, thin orange bill
with black tip

White breast
and belly with
black spots

Orange-pink legs

*"Peet-weet."
This soft call is made when
flying away from danger.*

Teeter-Totter Shorebirds

Up and down, teeter-totter, Spotted Sandpipers bob their tail as they pick and glean insects, snails
and crayfish along the Northeast's shorelines. The reason for the tail bobbing is a mystery. We do
know both chicks and adults bob their tails. At the least alarm, the motion may increase until the
entire lower half of the bird's body is in a fast teeter-totter. With a little more alarm, the bird may take
to the air calling *peet-weet-weet*. This action by Spotted Sandpipers is repeated along shorelines in
spring and summer. With a buddy, binoculars and bird watching manners, explore bird playgrounds
near you for teeter-tottering sandpipers!

Habitat Café

Yumm . . . bring an order of aquatic (water) and land insects, tadpoles, small frogs, mollusks and crayfish. Spotted Sandpipers are omnivorous.

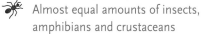

SPRING, SUMMER, FALL, WINTER MENU:
Almost equal amounts of insects, amphibians and crustaceans

Today's Special
grasshoppers

Life Cycle

NEST Both parents build the 5-inch-diameter nest in a shallow depression in the ground, hidden under grass or a small bush and lined with dry grass.

EGGS About 1¼ inches long. Dad is the main caregiver for the clutch of 4 eggs, which hatch in 20–21 days. A rarity in the bird world, females often mate with more than one male and lay eggs in up to five different nests.

MOM! DAD! Precocial. As soon as the chicks hatch, they walk to shore, usually with Dad—wee balls of bobbing fluff. They don't have tails at this point, just tiny rumps of fuzz. Their gray down is nearly invisible against pebbles and gravel. When in danger they flatten, becoming a part of the beach, or hurry to the water and dive for cover. One of the parents will spread its wings around the brood during the first week to keep the chicks warm and safe.

FLEDGLING Flight becomes routine when they are just weeks old.

JUVENILE At one year of age the birds are mature enough to date, mate and raise their own young.

Did You Know?

Spotted Sandpipers change their fashion each season. Just before fall migration, Spotted Sandpipers become unspotted. They molt, or lose their old feathers, and grow in new white feathers without spots. Their bill and legs turn to a dull yellow color during the winter. When it is time for spring and the nesting season to begin, they molt into spotted feathers again!

When

Spotted Sandpipers are diurnal. They feed during the day and rest at night.

Migration

Spring Arrival: Apr–May
Fall Departure: Jul–Sep
Short- to long-distance migrant. Solitary (alone) bird, even in migration. Migrates by night to wintering areas in southern US and as far south as Bolivia and Brazil.

Nesting

Spotted Sandpipers nest in late May–June in the Northeastern US.

Getting Around

Spotted Sandpipers fly directly up from shore in a burst of takeoff energy. In flight, their wings are stiff and flap only halfway up. This gives them their short, flickering flight. Look for their white wing stripe in flight. They dive straight into the water for safety and then straight out again from underneath the water!

Where to Look

Spotted Sandpipers live along shorelines of lakes, ponds, streams, rivers and wetlands.

Year-round	Summer
Migration	Winter

Red-winged Blackbird

Agelaius phoeniceus

Length: 7–9 inches (17–19 cm)
Wingspan: 12–16 inches (31–40 cm)

Males are
glossy black

Females have a light
eyebrow stripe; they are
brown above with streaks
of brown below

Red shoulder patch
with a yellow border

It takes young males
two years to become
black like Dad—called
"delayed maturation"

"O-ka-leee!"
means "Guys, stay away
from my territory! But
gals come on over—I have
room for 3 or 4."

Safety in Numbers

Red-winged Blackbirds practice safety in numbers. (It's harder for predators to capture prey in a large group.) In late summer, redwings attend the annual family reunion with their cousins: starlings, grackles and cowbirds. Look for a flying river of blackbirds above the fields and across the sky at dawn and dusk in September to November. It can take more than 10 minutes for a massive flock of 10,000 birds to pass. Flocks feed in the fields during the day and roost at night. Female redwings migrate south in the fall before males. In the spring, males return first to the Northeast's wetlands and roadsides to perch on a cattail, spread their red wing patches, and sing, "O-ka-lee . . . "

Habitat Café

Today's Special
snails

Yumm . . . bring an order of dragonflies, grasshoppers, spiders, beetles, moths and seeds like sunflowers. Their slender brown bill is designed to pick up insects and seeds. Red-winged Blackbirds are omnivorous.

SPRING, SUMMER MENU:
Mainly insects, some seeds and berries

FALL, WINTER MENU:
More seeds and berries, fewer insects than during spring and summer

Life Cycle

NEST The female builds the nest cup 3–10 feet above the ground in cattails, reeds and bushes over or near water. She weaves the leaves of water plants through the cattail stalks to make a nest cup. The inside of the nest is lined with soft, fine grasses.

EGGS About 1 inch long. The female incubates the 3–4 blue-green eggs with brown markings for 11 days.

MOM! DAD! Altricial. The female feeds the young and removes the fecal sacs (chick diapers) from the nest. If a predator comes too close to the nest, the female does a "flip-wing act" 5–10 feet from the nest.

NESTLING The chicks' eyes open when they are about one week old.

FLEDGLING Both parents feed the young for up to two weeks after they leave the nest.

JUVENILE Juveniles join a flock with other "teens." They feed during the day and roost at night. By fall they join a large group of both males and females and prepare to migrate to wintering areas.

Do the Math

Red-winged Blackbird chicks are fed insects. Insects are much higher in muscle and bone-building protein than seeds and berries. A male chick will increase in size by ten times in its first ten days. Multiply your birth weight by ten and you would be huge in only ten days. Do the math! But then, you don't need to grow into an adult your first year like a Red-winged Blackbird does. Answer on pages 194-195.

When
Red-winged Blackbirds are diurnal. They feed during the day and rest at night.

Migration
Spring Arrival: late Feb–Apr
Fall Departure: Sep–Nov
Short- to long-distance migrant. Red-winged Blackbirds gather in large groups of up to 100,000 birds before migrating to the southern US and as far south as Mexico and South America.

Nesting
Red-winged Blackbirds begin nesting in the Northeastern US during April and May.

Getting Around
Look for the Northeast's most common summer roadside bird sitting on top of signs, mile markers and fence posts. They walk on the ground to search for seeds and insects. Redwings fly in a pattern of closing their wings, dipping down, then rising again with a few wingbeats.

Where to Look
Red-winged Blackbirds are found in all of the Northeastern US; look for them in wet roadsides and fields, marshes and along the reedy edges of lakes and shores.

Year-round | Summer
Migration | Winter

Piping Plover

Charadrius melodus

Length: 7 inches (17 cm)
Wingspan: 19 inches (48 cm)

Black band
across forehead
from eye to eye

Single black
neck band

Sand colored above,
white underneath

Short, stout
orange bill
with black tip

White band across entire
tail seen in flight

Male and female
look alike

Color-coded bands may
be attached to a plover's
legs; scientists tag plovers
to learn about them and to
help protect them

"Kee-ah, kee-ah" means
the plover feels vulnerable
and is using its valuable
energy to convince you to
leave—skedaddle!

Threatened Species in the East

Piping Plover chicks scoot back and forth from the high beach to the tide line where they find insects to eat. They are unable to fly until they are about a month old, making this a very vulnerable period. The mere size of a golf or tennis ball, Piping Plover chicks are no match for vehicles, hungry cats, unleashed dogs and other predators. Nesting and living on the same beaches that people use for recreation is an ongoing challenge for the survival of the threatened Piping Plover. To keep them from extinction, keep your distance, carry out your beach trash, keep pets indoors or on a leash, follow the rules, support the experts in their research and pitch in when asked.

Habitat Café

Today's Special
bristleworms

Yumm . . . bring an order of marine worms, beetles, small marine animals and crustaceans with a side order of mollusks peppered with fly larvae. Piping Plovers are carnivorous, they eat only animal matter. Plovers make a quick series of run and peck when foraging for prey. They will also hold a foot forward and vibrate it on the top of the wet sand. Foot trembling may bring prey to the surface.

SPRING, SUMMER, FALL, WINTER MENU:
Marine insects, crustaceans, mollusks

Life Cycle

NEST The male puts on a pre-nesting party. Strutting around his territory, he tosses pebbles and shell pieces. He bends down and leans forward on his chest, moves back and forth, and kicks back sand, calling, "pipe-pipe-pipe." The female lays the eggs in a nest scrape generally away from water near a stone, a log, or a small clump of grass.

EGGS About 1¼ inch long. The clutch of 3–4 eggs is incubated by both parents for about 25–27 days. After hatching, the chicks whistle very softly to their parents.

MOM! DAD! Precocial. The downy chicks stay near the nest for a few days to be kept warm by their parents. With feathers the color of sand and pebbles, they are nearly invisible. If parents call out an alarm, the chicks lay flat with their head down. If they are on the move, one parent leads the chicks away while the other pretends to be injured.

FLEDGLING The chicks fly at about 30 days after hatching.

JUVENILE Juveniles may stay with their family until they migrate south. On their spring return they may start their own family of pipers.

Did You Know?

Piping Plovers are so important that they have their own US recovery team. We are a part of the extended team. Some states, like Delaware, are looking for volunteers to join the Piping Plover Monitoring team. Clue your teacher and family into the needs of this fascinating bird and explore the special Piping Plover activities at http://www.fws.gov/northeast/pipingplover/index.html. Let's pitch in by respecting the plover's need for undisturbed, protected spaces on the beach and telling others about their needs. Go team!

When

Diurnal. Piping Plovers are active during the day and rest at night.

Migration
Spring Arrival: Mar–Apr
Fall Departure: Aug–mid-Sep
Short- to mid-distance migrant in small groups to coastal beaches from North Carolina south on the Atlantic and Gulf Coasts. The greatest numbers of Piping Plovers winter in Texas.

Nesting
Piping Plovers begin nest construction in March–April in the Northeastern US. Listen for their bell-like, piping whistles for a signal that they are back from migration and ready to nest.

Getting Around
Piping Plovers in the Northeast spend most of their time walking and running with short stops along the beaches of the Atlantic Ocean. They are well camouflaged against the sand. When in flight, look for their bright white underside.

Where to Look
The open sandy beaches of the Atlantic coast, especially above tide line and often close to sand dunes. Preferred areas have access to salt ponds, temporary pools and bays.

| Year-round | Summer |
| Migration | Winter |

Belted Kingfisher

Megaceryle alcyon

Length: 11–14 inches (28–35 cm)
Wingspan: 19–23 inches (48–58 cm)

female

Females wear a rusty-orange-colored belt

Head crest can stick straight up or stay closer to the head

Juveniles look like adults but with a much smaller bill

Blue-gray above with a white throat collar and a blue band across the chest

Males do not have a belt

"Rattle, rattle, rattle . . ." This rattle call echoes against stream banks and riverbanks.

Expert Anglers

Scan the telephone wires and tree branches over a stream or river for the big-crested head and broad bill of this expert angler. Then sit quietly and watch as the blue-gray kingfisher studies the shallow, clear water for the movement of small fish, frogs and crayfish. Once it spots dinner, it dives like an arrow, plunging its bill into the water. Captured! The prey is taken back to the perch where the kingfisher shakes its head and pounds the fish. This stuns the fish, breaking the bones of sticklebacks and bullheads, and the kingfisher turns the fish and swallows it headfirst. The kingfisher's two-part stomach is not equipped for scales and bones. Instead, these hard-to-digest items are formed into a pellet and coughed up.

Habitat Café

Today's Special

leopard frogs

Yumm . . . bring an order of tadpoles, small fish, crayfish and dragonflies. Belted Kingfishers are carnivorous. They most often eat small fish that live in shallow water or stay near the surface. A kingfisher uses its thick pincher bill to catch prey. Look for its white wing patches in flight.

SPRING, SUMMER, FALL, WINTER MENU:
Fish, frogs, tadpoles and aquatic insects

Life Cycle

NEST Both the male and female dig out a tunnel just a few feet from the top of a river or stream bank, a sand or gravel pit, or bluff. At the end of the 3- to 15-foot tunnel is a nesting room. The eggs are laid on fish bones and scales from spit-up food pellets that have fallen apart.

EGGS About 1¼ inches long. The female incubates the clutch of 6–7 eggs for 22–24 days. Dad sits in when Mom takes a break.

MOM! DAD! Altricial. Both parents bring a wad of regurgitated fish to feed the chicks during the first days.

NESTLING More like a cat in a litter box than a bird, nestlings back up and shoot their feces on the wall. They turn around and hammer soil from over the top of the wall with their bills.

FLEDGLING At four weeks of age, Mom or Dad sits on a nearby perch with a fish in its bill. When the chicks are hungry enough, they come out. Parents feed them less often as they grow.

JUVENILE Juveniles take ten days of fishing lessons. Their parents drop dead fish in the water for the young to capture.

Unsolved Mystery

What kind of fish did the kingfisher eat for dinner last week? To solve this mystery, first find their perch and look underneath for pellets. Inside the pellets are the answers to their recent menu. You may find bones and scales that will help you identify the species of fish they ate. You can even tell how old the fish were by counting the rings on the scales!

When

Kingfishers are diurnal. They feed during the day and rest at night.

Migration

Spring Arrival: Mar–Apr
Fall Departure: Sep–Nov
Short- to long-distance migrants as far south as Central or South America. Some may overwinter in the Northeast where open water remains.

Nesting

They begin to dig the nest burrow in April with incubation generally in May–June in the Northeastern US near salt water or fresh water where there are suitable banks or cliffs.

Getting Around

Kingfishers perch on a branch, rock outcrop or on a wire over a river, stream, or lake. Once they spot prey, they dive headfirst, catching it in their large bill. They also hover over an area for a short time to catch prey. Their short legs and feet with joined toes are not adapted for walking. They only need their feet for shuffling in and out of their burrow and perching.

Where to Look

Along the Northeast's streams, rivers, wooded creeks, ponds, lakes and marine bays and estuaries.

Year-round	Summer
Migration	Winter

Pied-billed Grebe

Podilymbus podiceps

Length: 12–15 inches (30–38 cm)
Wingspan: 18–24½ inches (45–62 cm)

winter

White eye-rings look
like sunglasses with
a fake nose

Square-ish,
flat head

Dark brown all over
with a white patch
underneath

White bill with a black
ring around the middle

Females and males look
similar; males are larger

Flat, green, partially
webbed (lobed) toes
and feet

"Kuk-kuk-kuk-kuk-kuk-kuk-kuk, cow-cow-uh, cow-uh, cow-uh-cow-uh." Call begins soft and slow, but ends loud and fast.

Mini-submarines

Where did it go? Sinking in the water like a sneaky submarine, a Pied-billed Grebe can keep you waiting for its return. With their periscope eyes and camouflaged black and white bill, the only parts above the water, they can stay hidden for a long time. The trick to sinking in the water at just the right level is the grebe's ability to force out and control the amount of air held in its feathers and body. Typical of diving birds, their legs are far back on their body and their wings are small. Don't let their small size fool you. They can sneak up on other birds in fierce attacks to claim their territory and protect their young. There it is—gone again!

Habitat Café

Yumm . . . bring an order of fish, dragonflies and nymphs, beetles, bugs, snails, mussels, frogs and crayfish. Their chicken-like, arched bill is just right for catching prey or crushing crustaceans. Pied-billed Grebes are both *insectivores* and *carnivores*.

Today's Special
Snails

SPRING, SUMMER, FALL, WINTER MENU:

 Equal amounts of fish and insects, some crustaceans

Life Cycle

NEST As soon as the winter ice is melted, the female and male build their nest on a floating mat of decayed vegetation held to plant stalks in water at least 1 foot deep.

EGGS About 1¾ inches long. The female incubates the clutch of 4–8 eggs for just 23 days. She covers the eggs with a layer of plant leaves when she takes a break.

MOM! DAD! Precocial. Chicks can leave the nest for brief periods as soon as they are dry. They are in danger of drowning so they hitch a ride on the back of Mom and Dad. This cozy ride also protects them from predators. In only a few weeks, these little black-and-white striped "water skunks" can swim, dive and sink like their parents.

FLEDGLING The young grebes are able to fly and become independent when they are 8–9 weeks of age.

JUVENILE On their spring migration return, they are mature enough to date, mate and raise their own young.

Gross Factor

Grebes eat their own feathers throughout their lifetime, at times filling nearly half their stomach capacity. Parents feed feathers to their chicks soon after hatching. Biologists theorize that the feathers act to strain the stomach contents, preventing fish bones from passing into the intestines. Periodically, grebes spit up pellets of undigested feathers and other hard matter. Gross!

When

Pied-billed Grebes are diurnal. Normally, they are active during the day and rest at night. But during migration they are shy, nighttime fliers.

Migration

Spring Arrival: Mar–Apr
Fall Departure: Sep–Nov
Short- to mid-distance migrant wintering in the southern United States and northern Mexico. They overwinter in open lakes, river estuaries and tidal creeks to the south.

Nesting

Pied-billed Grebes begin nesting as soon as the winter ice is melted, generally in late April and May.

Getting Around

Being wary birds, Pied-billed Grebes crash-dive into the water when they sense danger. This causes a spray of water several feet into the air, blocking the vision of the predator. By the time the spray is gone, so is the sneaky grebe!

Where to Look

Pied-billed Grebes live in wetlands, shallow lakes and ponds that have dense stands of cattails and open water. They are listed as a threatened species in Massachusetts.

Year-round	Summer
Migration	Winter

Wetlands, Rivers, Lakes and Shores Habitat 165

Hooded Merganser

Lophodytes cucullatus

Length: 16–19 inches (40–49 cm)
Wingspan: 23½–26 inches (60–66 cm)

female

Bright yellow eye (female, brownish eye)

Long, narrow saw-toothed (serrated) bill

Male raises his white, fan-shaped crest during courtship displays

In flight, black and white on triangular-shaped wings

"Craaa-crrrooooo." Nicknamed the frog duck, males make this frog-like call during breeding season to attract a gal.

Divers of the Northeast

Hooded Mergansers are diving ducks that eat water insects, fish and crayfish in the wooded ponds, rivers and freshwater wetlands of the Northeast. They find their next meal with the aid of expert vision and feet that work like a water propulsion engine. Merganser's eyes have special lenses that readily adapt to differing light conditions, from those found in the open air to the light levels underwater. Their webbed feet have an extra paddle, a broad outer toe called a lobed hallux, that propels them through water. Hooded Mergansers stay in the Northeast in the fall until the water freezes. While they are spending winter to the south, you can build a nest box, hang it on a tree in their habitat and watch for their spring return.

Habitat Café

Yumm . . . bring an order of aquatic insects and fish with a heaping side order of crayfish. Hooded Mergansers are omnivorous, they eat both plant and animal matter. They use their slender, saw-toothed bill for grasping and holding onto wiggly prey.

SPRING, SUMMER, FALL, WINTER MENU:
Aquatic insects, fish and crustaceans

Today's Special *Crayfish*

Life Cycle

NEST Hooded Mergansers nest in the cavities of living or dead trees near water. They will also nest in a nest box with a 4 x 5 inch opening. Females construct a shallow bowl with materials already in the nest and then add a lining of down feathers.

EGGS About 2 inches long. Females incubate the clutch of 10–12 eggs for about 29–33 days. Females break up the long hours of 24/7 incubation by taking recesses.

MOM! DAD! Precocial. Covered with down, the chicks are ready to leave the nest within the first 24 hours of hatching. Mom checks the area, gives the OK to come down from the nest, *croo-croo-crook*, and the ducklings make a leap to the ground. They feed by peering under the water and diving for aquatic insects. If need be, Mom will power herself across the water with her wings in a broken wing display to lure a predator away from the ducklings.

FLEDGLING The young can fly between 2 and 3 months of age.

JUVENILE The young are able to mate and raise their own young at 2 years of age.

Did You Know?

How many eyelids do birds have? Three. They have an upper and lower lid and a third, usually clear, lid between the two lids and the cornea. The third lid is the nictitating membrane. This lid is used for blinking and keeps their eyes clean, moist and protected from their chicks while they feed them. In loons and other diving birds, the nictitating membrane has a clear center, which acts like a pair of goggles underwater.

When

Diurnal. Hooded Mergansers are active during the day and rest at night.

Migration
Spring Arrival: Mar
Fall Departure: Oct–Nov
Short-distance migrant south along the Atlantic Coast as far as Florida. Hooded Mergansers stay put in the Northeastern US as long as they can between the spring ice melt and winter ice up.

Nesting
Hooded Mergansers begin nesting as early as March in the Northeastern US.

Getting Around
Hooded Mergansers use fast and nearly constant wingbeats in flight, only stopping to glide when landing. They ski across the water's surface with their feet held forward to break their landing.

Where to Look
In the Northeast, Hooded Mergansers can be found near wooded freshwater wetlands, streams and ponds with plenty of shrub cover to hide the wandering young.

Year-round	Summer
Migration	Winter

Wood Duck

Aix sponsa

Length: 18½–21½ inches (47–54)
Wingspan: 26–29 inches (66–73 cm)

female

Female is brown; its breast is white streaked above, gray below; white eye patch and throat, with a bushy, pointed crest

Red eye and eye-ring

Yellow and red bill with a black tip

Iridescent green head and slicked back crest

Long, dark tail held at upright angle

White throat, chin collar and strap

"Jeeb!" is a whistle made by male Wood Ducks. Females call "Oo-eek, oo-eek" to their broods, and often give the call while in flight.

Another Success Story

Wood Ducks need habitat. They need trees with holes for nesting, food, shelter and nearby water. Drain wetland habitat, harvest older woodland trees and hunt more ducks than can be raised each year and Wood Ducks become rare. By the early 1900s, this was the case in the US. The good news? Wildlife biologists studied the needs of Wood Ducks and came up with a plan. Nest boxes were built and placed near wetlands, lakes and rivers with the help of sporting groups and individuals. Data was kept on the young that hatched. The number of Wood Ducks that hunters were allowed to harvest each year was regulated. The plan worked. Today, Wood Ducks are all over the region. Success happens.

Today's Special

acorns and dragonflies

Habitat Café

Yumm . . . bring an order of seeds and tender shoots of aquatic (water) plants, fruit and nuts, insects and snails. Wood Ducks have a stretchy esophagus and store food. A researcher found a duck with 30 acorns in its esophagus! Wood Ducks are omnivorous.

SPRING, SUMMER, FALL MENU:
Almost entirely plant matter, some animal matter

WINTER MENU:
Mostly seeds and acorns, more animal matter than summer

Life Cycle

NEST The female makes the nest in a tree cavity or woodpecker hole, 6–30 feet above ground and near a wetland, a small lake, or river. She lines the nest with her down feathers. Build a nest box lined with wood chips and place it in Wood Duck habitat. Check it regularly.

EGGS About 2 inches long. The female incubates the clutch of 10–15 eggs for 25–35 days. Several females may all lay 30–40 eggs in just ONE nest box. One lucky hen will incubate all of the eggs!

MOM! DAD! Precocial. Hatched with eyes open, with warm, brown and yellow down and sharp toenails. After a day of fluffing out, they climb to the edge of the nesting hole, pop out and float to the ground. Mom calls an OK signal, "kuk, kuk, kuk," and watches without helping. She leads her waddling puffballs to the nearest water. Mom keeps them warm at night for the first month. Young birds are able to fly and become independent at 7–10 weeks old.

JUVENILE Juveniles group in late summer to early fall. A female picks her mate on the southern wintering grounds. The chosen male follows her back to her original nesting area to make their new home.

Birding Tip

Is the duck stuck? No, the duck with its rump sticking up from the water is a dabbling duck. There are two groups of ducks: dabblers and divers. Dabblers tip up as they reach down through shallow water with their bill to forage for food on the bottom. Just under the surface their webbed feet paddle to keep them partly under water. Wood Ducks and Mallards are dabbling ducks.

When

Wood Ducks are diurnal. They feed during the day and rest at night.

Migration
Spring Arrival: Mar–May
Fall Departure: Sep–Nov
Short-distance migrant to the southern United States and Mexico. A few hardy Wood Ducks overwinter in the region.

Nesting
Wood Ducks begin nesting in late March–April in the Northeast in nest boxes or natural tree cavities near water. They will reuse Pileated Woodpecker and Northern Flicker nest cavities also.

Getting Around
Wood Ducks fly straight and fast into their nesting hole—without bumping their head! They walk along the water's edge to feed. In the water, they are excellent swimmers. They dive to escape predators. Takeoff from the water is quick and straight up with very fast wingbeats.

Where to Look
Wooded habitat along rivers, streams and small lakes and swamps across the Northeast.

Year-round	Summer
Migration	Winter

American Oystercatcher

Haematopus palliatus

Length: 16–17½ inches (40–44 cm)
Wingspan: 32 inches (81 cm)

Black head

Yellow eyes with red eye-ring

Brown above and white below

Females are larger than males

Long, bright red bill is narrow from side to side

Bold white stripe in wings visible in flight

Long, pink legs

"Kleep, kleep, kleep." Both males and females use this call to say, "I am here!"

Tools of the Trade

The tools of the trade for this beach-dweller are a chisel, shovel, lever, knife and hammer. A master 'craftsbird' of locating and opening prey, the Oystercatcher uses its bright red bill like a hammer to dislodge a mussel from a reef. It continues to hammer it on just the right spot until the shell opens. The reward is a soft tasty meal inside. To bring a clam from the sand, the bird loosens the sand with a lever-and-shovel action and then strategically stabs its bill in the spot where the membrane chain holds the two sides together. The oystercatcher also chisels open a clam or oyster by pivoting its bill sideways. Another juicy meal waits.

Habitat Café

Today's Special
oysters

Yumm . . . bring an order of mussels, clams, oysters and sandworms. American Oystercatchers are carnivorous, they eat animal matter.

SPRING, SUMMER, FALL, WINTER MENU:
Shellfish and other invertebrates

Life Cycle

NEST Oystercatchers spend little time or effort in building a nest. They simply settle on the sand and make a shallow scrape with their feet. A rim of broken shells may be added.

EGGS About 2 inches long. Both parents incubate the clutch of 2–4 eggs for about 27 days.

MOM! DAD! Precocial. The downy chicks can stand and run just hours after hatching but are dependent on their parents for food for the next 2 months until their amazing bill is fully developed. Mom and Dad find shellfish and open and remove the soft inner flesh for the young. The food may be delivered in pieces or in liquid form brought back up from the parents' stomach and funneled into the chicks open bill.

FLEDGLING The chicks' first flights begin at 35 days of age.

JUVENILE Juveniles fly with their family to wintering areas and stay with them until they are about 6 months of age. They may pair up in their first 2 years and defend territories, but they are not mature enough to successfully mate and lay eggs until they are 3–4 years of age.

Birding Tip

American Oystercatcher pairs have a dating bird-bop. The birds run side by side with heads bopping up and down while giving a piping call. They may continue this in flight with other pairs, called a dating tournament. If you find yourself on an Atlantic beach with an oystercatcher circling right above you with deep, slow wingbeats, it may be luring you away from its nest and young.

When

Diurnal. American Oystercatchers are active during the day and rest at night.

Migration
Spring Arrival: Mar–Apr
Fall Departure: Aug–Sep
Short-distance migrant in large flocks to wintering areas from Virginia south along the Atlantic coast. Some overwinter along the Atlantic coast of the Northeastern US. They roost in winter groups of 50–100 oystercatchers.

Nesting
American Oystercatchers begin nest construction in April in the Northeastern US.

Getting Around
Oystercatchers spend most of their time walking or running on the beach. When they do fly, they use deep and rapid wingbeats. To rest, they stand on one or both legs and tuck their bill in their wing feathers.

Where to Look
In the Northeast, American Oystercatchers are found on sand and shell beaches, dunes and salt marshes along the Atlantic coast from Boston south to Florida. They have wandered as far north as Maine.

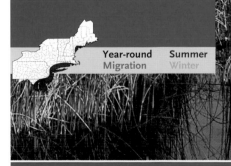

Year-round	Summer
Migration	Winter

Ring-billed Gull

Larus delawarensis

Length: 17–21½ inches(43–54 cm)
Wingspan: 41½–46 inches (105–117 cm)

winter

Yellow bill with a black "ring" near the tip

White body

Gray wings

Look for black wingtips with white spots

Yellow legs and feet

Females and males look the same

"Keeeeeaaaah—kah, kah, kah, kah, kah!"

Swashbuckling Pirates of the Air

Ahoy! The pirates of the bird world, Ring-billed Gulls pillage food treasures and fill their coffers with loot from ships that dump garbage overboard, as well as from landfills, parking lots, city parks, plowed fields, and along roads and beaches. Ring-bills are opportunists, eating nearly anything: fish, rodents, small aquatic animals, insects, bird chicks and eggs, and even fruit and fast food leftovers. These swashbuckling gulls will steal fish right out of the bills of water birds like mergansers and snatch fish from the surface of the water. Use your spyglass to watch these flying pirates.

Habitat Café

Today's Special
human food, garbage

Yumm . . . bring an order of fish, insects, spiders, earthworms and waste grains (corn). Ring-billed Gulls are omnivorous. They eat both plant and animal matter.

SPRING, SUMMER, FALL, WINTER MENU:
🐟 Animal and plant matter

Life Cycle

NEST The nest is on a beach or island in the open ground on matted plants or in rocks. Ring-billed gulls nest in a group called a colony. Champion recyclers, they may even line their nest with garbage.

EGGS Slightly more than 2¼ inches long. The female incubates the clutch of 2–3 eggs for 20–23 days.

MOM! DAD! Semi-precocial. Chicks blend into the shore with mottled brown, gray, or white down on their backs and white bellies. They can swim at 3–5 days of age. Lunch includes recycled food that their parents ate and then spit up near the nest. Scrumptious!

NESTLING With so many chicks and adults in a colony, how do they tell each other apart? Mom and Dad can pick out their chicks in a crowd of young by their unique facial markings. Chicks know their own parents' calls when they are 4–5 days of age.

FLEDGLING Young birds fledge when they are 3–5 weeks of age and leave the family group when they are able to fly.

JUVENILE The ring on their bill develops at 1 year of age and adult plumage (feather color and pattern) at 3 years of age.

Unsolved Mystery

Do birds play, or are all their actions related to survival? Watch gulls as they drop an object and swoop down to pick it up, drop the object and swoop to pick it up, drop the object . . . over and over. Are they practicing catching prey, or playing a game for fun? Go ahead, play with this unsolved mystery!

When

Ring-billed Gulls are diurnal, active during the day and resting at night.

Migration

Spring Arrival: Mar–Apr
Fall Departure: Sep–Nov
Short- to mid-distance migrant to lakes, rivers, landfills, golf courses, fields and parks in the southern US and northern Mexico. Ring-billed gulls do not depend on open water or specific foods and come back north earlier than many other shorebirds. Some even stay all year.

Nesting

Ring-billed Gulls begin nesting in May in the Northeastern US.

Getting Around

Ring-billed Gulls walk along the shore in a side-to-side stride with attitude! Look for their wings held in a "V" shape as they land on water. Floating atop the water like a buoy, they dip their head under for food. In the air, they are strong fliers and also hover and soar on thermals.

Where to Look

Ring-billed Gulls prefer islands, rock reefs and marshes, but they will visit areas on land near people too.

Year-round Summer
Migration   Winter

Mallard

Anas platyrhynchos

Length: 20–25½ inches (50–65 cm)
Wingspan: 32½–37½ inches (82–95 cm)

female

Females, or hens, are streaked brown with an orange bill with small black spots; the speculum, a band of wing color, is metallic blue edged with white

Male (drake) has a green head with a white neck ring and a red-brown chest

Male has a black tail curl

Orange, webbed feet paddle water and push the body down to reach plants

"Quack, quack" is made only by females. Males have two calls of their own, a nasal warning "rhaeb" and a short courtship whistle.

From Marshes to Malls—Mallards Are All Over!

Mallards are *Super Adaptors*! In cities, they have been seen nesting in downtown flower planters and balconies of buildings. Close to people or not, as long as there is shallow water and food nearby, Mallards are content. They eat everything from insects to frogs, plants that live under and on top of water, seeds from farm crops and wild plants. Watch for Mallards eating cracked corn under bird feeders. Mallards are also big eaters of mosquito larvae and pupae that live on the top of shallow water. With Mallards near, you can enjoy being outdoors with fewer mosquitoes to swat.

Habitat Café

Yumm . . . bring an order of seeds and shoots of aquatic plants, grass, snails, worms and insects. Mallards are omnivorous. They eat both plant and animal matter.

Today's Special
wild rice and corn

SPRING BREEDING SEASON MENU:
Lots of insects and animal matter

SUMMER, FALL MENU:
Includes aquatic plants and seeds

WINTER MENU:
Can include grains from farm crops

Life Cycle

NEST Built near water at the base of tall wetland plants or under a woody shrub. The female makes a few scrapes in the ground and lays her eggs. She then adds grass, reeds and leaves from nearby plants to make a nest rim around her body. Soft down feathers line the inside.

EGGS About 2¼ inches long. The female incubates the clutch of 9–13 eggs for 26–30 days.

MOM! DAD! Precocial. Mallard ducklings hatch covered with fluffy down and their eyes fully open. Mom is on her own with her large brood. The hatchlings are out of the nest after the first day and follow her to water.

Mallards dive for food during the first weeks after hatching, but this behavior disappears with the arrival of their flight feathers. Until they can fly at two months of age, they still need Mom's protection from snapping turtles, bass and raccoons.

JUVENILE At 10 weeks of age, young Mallards leave the family group to join a mixed flock of adults and juveniles. When they return in the spring, they are mature enough to raise their own family.

Did You Know?

While Mom is taking care of the ducklings, Dad joins a flock and stays very quiet. Male Mallards molt, or lose the old feathers and grow new ones, before fall migration. The bright breeding season feathers are replaced by dull camouflaged brown feathers called "eclipse plumage." During this time, they are unable to fly for a short period until the new feathers grow in.

When

Diurnal. They feed during the day and rest at night.

Migration

Spring Arrival: Mar–Apr
Fall Departure: Sep–Nov
Short- to mid-distance migrant to the southern United States and Mexico. Some Mallards stay in the Northeastern US during the winter, wherever they find suitable open water within a reasonable "commuting distance" of feeding areas.

Nesting

Mallards begin nesting in the Northeast in late April–May.

Getting Around

Mallards are strong and direct fliers capable of reaching speeds up to 45–60 miles per hour. When they are alarmed they can spring straight up from the water. They use their wings and feet as brakes when making a landing into water! Mallards are also excellent swimmers.

Where to Look

Lakes, wetlands, rivers, parks and farm ponds. Explore city, county and state parks, and public areas or nature centers. Mallards may even eat cracked corn under bird feeders!
· *Super Adaptor*

| Year-round | Summer |
| Migration | Winter |

Osprey

Pandion haliaetus

Length: 21½–23 inches (54–58 cm)
Wingspan: 59–71 inches (150–180 cm)

White crown
and forehead

Dark line
through eye

Long wings
with dark patch
at bend in wing

Brown back and
upper wings

Mostly white
breast and belly

The female is larger
than the male, and
generally has a
more marked band
of brown feathers
across the breast

" Tiooop, tioooop, tiooop."
Males and females make this
whistle call when guarding
the nest.

Olympic-style Adaptations . . .

Ospreys dive in and escape with the prize—however wiggly and slippery it may be. They have Olympic-style adaptations for surviving along waterways. Equipped with feathers so closely spaced and well oiled they are waterproof, they race into the clear water feet first to pluck their prize from the top few feet. Long and curved talons, barbed foot pads and reversible outer toes secure the desperate fish. If that isn't enough, two toes positioned forward and two backward lock the fish in a headfirst hold that makes for an aerodynamic getaway. Take to the waterways and cheer the performance of this wild champion.

Habitat Café

Yumm.. bring an order of fresh, wiggling, living fish, with a side order of fish. Ospreys are carnivorous. They dive feet first in shallow water for fish. Their catch is taken to a perch, often near the nest, where it is devoured with enthusiasm.

SPRING, SUMMER, FALL, WINTER MENU:

🐟 Fish

Today's Special
fresh juicy fish

Life Cycle

NEST Ospreys build their nest on top of a tall living or dead tree or a cliff along lakes and streams. They have also adapted to nesting on nest poles placed close to water. The male brings in large sticks for the base and smaller sticks, grass and wetland materials for the inside. To keep the eggs from falling through cracks, the female adds flat objects last. Once a sturdy nest is built, the pair may reuse it year to year.

EGGS About 2½ inches long. The female incubates the clutch of 1–4 eggs for 37 days.

MOM! DAD! Semiprecocial. The downy young beg loudly with the prize (food) going to the loudest. The third chick to hatch is generally smaller than the first chicks, making survival a challenge.

FLEDGLING At 7 weeks of age, the young exercise their wings at the nest rim and then leave the nest.

JUVENILE Ospreys do not leave their wintering areas until their second or third spring when they often return to the area where they were raised. They are mature enough at 3–5 years of age to nest.

Did You Know?

Ospreys are near the top of the lake food chain. In the 1950s, pesticides leaked into water supplies and were absorbed by fish that were in turn eaten by Osprey. The chemicals weakened the shells of their eggs and fewer chicks hatched. The Osprey population plummeted. With the banning of some pesticides, the number of Ospreys in the Northeast has steadily increased but it remains a species to keep a close watch on. Welcome back!

When

Ospreys are diurnal, active during the day and resting at night.

Migration
Spring Arrival: late Mar–Apr
Fall Departure: late Aug–Oct
Mid- to long-distance migrant. Ospreys migrate by day south of the US to Central and South America. Females migrate earlier in the fall and travel farther than males.

Nesting
The male Osprey arrives before the female to locate the nest. They begin nesting in April and May in the Northeast region.

Getting Around
Look for the dark patch at the bend of their long, narrow wings. Flight is steady and rowing with stiff wingbeats. They soar high on thermals to save energy. Ospreys don't wear nose plugs when diving, but they almost do. Their nasal valves close and prevent them from drowning when they dive into water.

Where to Look
Ospreys fish in the clear, shallow waters along lakes, rivers, streams and coasts. Ospreys are a threatened species in some states.

Year-round	Summer
Migration	Winter

Common Loon

Gavia immer

Length: 26–36 inches (66–91 cm)
Wingspan: 41–51½ inches (104–131 cm)

Males and females molt
summer feathers to gray
winter plumage with
white below

Red eyes filter light
in deep water

Black head
and neck

White-striped
necklace

White breast,
black-and-white
checkered back

Wailing means "I'm over here, fellow loons!" This can sound like the howl of a wolf or an eerie laugh.

Bird of the Wilderness

Common Loons spend almost their entire lives on water. With hundreds of lakes and plenty of fish, the Common Loon makes itself at home in the northern lakes of the Northeastern US. During the winter their home is in the coastal waters of the Atlantic Ocean. Built for deep water diving, a loon flattens its feathers to push out air and become less buoyant. With its small, pointed wings to its sides, it plunges below the surface, paddling with webbed feet. In a short time, it strikes prey with its long, sharp bill partly open. Parents train their young to catch prey by dropping fish in front of them. Chicks ride along on their parents' backs. This protects the young from predators, and makes a great diving platform.

Today's Special

frogs and crayfish

Habitat Café

Yumm . . . bring an order of fish (perch, lake trout, bullheads), minnows and aquatic insects. Common Loons are carnivorous. How do loons hold on to slippery fish? Their tongue and the roof of their mouth have sharp points that face backward like the barb on the end of a fishhook. A loon's throat expands for eating large fish.

SPRING, SUMMER, FALL, WINTER MENU:
Lots of fish, a few insects

Life Cycle

NEST Loons will nest on a floating mat of plants attached to shoreline vegetation, close to the water on bare ground—even on a muskrat house. Parents add more plants to the 2-foot diameter nest during incubation.

EGGS About 3½ inches long. Both the female and male incubate the clutch of 2 eggs for 28 days.

MOM! DAD! Precocial. The downy young can dive up to 10 feet deep at only 10 days old. Riding on the back of Mom or Dad protects them from predators such as northern pike, muskies and bald eagles. The family moves farther away from motorboats and people to a nursery area, a quiet bay where the young birds have more protection from predators.

FLEDGLING Young do not fly until they are 12 weeks old. Both parents feed the chicks whole food for 2–3 months, even when the chicks can feed themselves at 6 weeks of age.

JUVENILE Juvenile loons migrate in flocks and may stay in wintering areas for their first 2 years. They are mature enough to date, mate and raise their own young when they are at least 4 years of age.

Birding Tip

Loons need large, deep lakes of 150–500 acres with space away from people and boats; they need about 200 yards of space (the length of two soccer fields) to launch themselves out of the water when taking flight. The loon makes a tremolo call when it is upset. Use a spotting scope, binoculars, or the zoom lens on your camera to view loons. Check with your state wildlife officials for information on being a volunteer loon watcher that reports nest locations and activity. Take action!

When ☀

Common Loons are diurnal, active during the day and resting at night.

Migration

Spring Arrival: late Mar–Jun
Fall Departure: Sep–Dec
Short- to mid-distance migrant to Atlantic coast from North Carolina to Florida and the Gulf of Mexico. Some overwinter along the coast of the Northeastern US. They flock on large lakes before migration. Juveniles leave 4–6 weeks after adults.

Nesting

Common Loons begin nesting in May in the Northeastern US.

Getting Around

Loons can dive 250 feet and stay underwater 5 minutes. Legs positioned far back on their body propel them in the water like a torpedo. They do not walk, but scoot on land and need a very large lake for a long water takeoff.

Where to Look

Common Loons live on deep lakes of 150–500 acres with islands or shorelines with vegetation during breeding season. Look along the Atlantic Ocean in the winter.

Year-round	Summer
Migration	Winter

Canada Goose

Branta canadensis

Length: 30–43½ inches (76–110 cm)
Wingspan: 50–67 inches (127–170 cm)

in flight

Bill: Small saw-like points on the edges of the upper and lower mandibles help the goose grip plants and strip seeds from standing grasses

gosling

Look for their white underside and dark tail when they take flight

Long, black neck with white throat patch

Females and males look similar, but the males are slightly larger

"Ha-roonk, ha-roonk!"

It's a Family Affair

Honk, honk . . . the family is touching down. For Canada Geese, it's a family affair from the time they hatch through their adulthood. During their first year, the young stay with their parents, traveling in a family flock that may join up with other family groups. When they are mature enough to start their own family at age 2–5 years, they pair up and stay with the same mate for life. Pairs return to the same breeding area each year and so do their daughters. The family group then continues to increase in a given area leading to some challenges in urban areas. Wildlife biologists and managers work toward balancing both the needs of wildlife and people.

Today's Special
field corn

Habitat Café

Yumm . . . bring an order of roots, stems, leaves, fruits, berries and seeds. Canada Geese are herbivores. They also like to eat bluegrass—the kind of grass found on lakeshore lawns and golf courses.

SPRING, SUMMER, FALL MENU:
Aquatic plants high in protein

WINTER MENU:
Grass, agricultural crops, fruit, berries and seeds

Life Cycle

NEST Geese nest on muskrat houses, beaver lodges and floating mats of vegetation, or build their own nest, usually on the ground.

It's best to stay far away from nests. Females will lay their neck flat and lie motionless on the nest. Males defend the nest with gusto. They have been known to attack intruders with their strong neck, bill and wings. Spotting scopes, binoculars and a camera with a zoom lens are great for safe, close-up views of wildlife!

EGGS About 3½ inches long. The female incubates the clutch of 4–7 eggs for 28 days. Dad sits on the nest when Mom takes a break.

MOM! DAD! Precocial. The down-covered goslings are able to walk, swim, feed and dive just one day after hatching. They instinctively spread their webbed feet out to push through the water and then close the web when the foot comes forward again. The goslings are fully fledged with strong flight feathers at 7–9 weeks of age.

JUVENILE Juveniles stay with their parents through the first year and are mature enough at 2–5 years of age to mate and raise their own young.

Birding Tip

Draw for Ducks! You can be a part of waterfowl conservation efforts by creating your own artwork featuring ducks in their natural habitat. Enter your artwork in the US Fish & Wildlife Service's Junior Duck Stamp Contest. Eligible species include Hooded Merganser (page 166–167), Mallard (page 174–175), Wood Duck (page 168–169) and Canada Goose. To learn more, visit www.fws.gov/juniorduck/ArtContest.htm.

When

Canada Geese are diurnal, active during the day and resting at night.

Migration
Spring Arrival: Feb–Apr
Fall Departure: Sept–Nov
Short-distance migrant to central and southern US. Many overwinter in the Northeast where they find open water, including the Chesapeake Bay and Delmarva region, and the Atlantic coastline from New York to New Jersey and inland to southern Pennsylvania.

Nesting
Canada Geese begin nesting in March–April in the Northeastern US.

Getting Around
Canada Geese can move fast for large birds, flying at speeds of 40–60 mph. Their "V" formation is energy efficient, too. Flying in the slipstream of the leader, the other geese face less wind resistance and use less energy. When the lead goose tires, it changes place with another goose. Now that's teamwork.

Where to Look
Canada Geese live in open country with wetlands, ponds and lakeshores—even golf courses and city parks.

| Year-round | Summer |
| Migration | Winter |

Great Egret

Ardea alba

Length: 3–3½ feet (94–104 cm)
Wingspan: 4½ feet (131–145 cm)

aigrettes

in flight

Long, sharp yellow bill designed for spearing fish

Yellow eyes

During breeding season the top of the bill to just below the eye is apple green

A very long neck

All-white bird with black legs and feet

Females and males look the same

"Frawnk" or, "Alarm!" When you hear this call, take the hint and move farther away.

Great Egrets Escape Fashion Fad

Egrets wear beautiful, long white feathers (aigrettes) on their backs during their spring courtship season. Women in the late 1800s to the early 1900s thought wearing aigrettes in their hats would be just as gorgeous. Overhunting to pluck the fashionable feathers from the egrets nearly led to their extinction. People took action just in time to protect egrets and other nongame birds worldwide with the Migratory Bird Treaty Act of 1918. Great Egrets recovered and began nesting in greater numbers again. Trek to a river floodplain, wetland, stream, island and shallow shores to watch Great Egrets feathered for the spring fashion show.

Habitat Café

Today's Special

giant water bugs

Yumm . . . bring an order of small fish, frogs, crayfish, dragonflies and whirligig beetles, tadpoles, snakes, lizards and small mammals. The long, sharp yellow bill is designed for spearing fish. Great Egrets are omnivorous.

SPRING, SUMMER, FALL, WINTER MENU:

 Mostly fish, with some reptiles, amphibians and insects

Life Cycle

NEST Both parents build the bulky, two-foot-diameter nest of sticks and twigs in trees 10–30 feet above ground. Great Egrets nest on their own or in colonies. Their feet have a special, long back toe to steady them while they perch in the nesting tree.

EGGS About 2¼ inches long. Both the male and female incubate the clutch of 3–4 eggs for 23–26 days.

MOM! DAD! Altricial. Both parents help feed the downy chicks.

NESTLING By the end of the first week, the chick's feathers begin to grow and are complete at 4–5 weeks of age. Like an umbrella, Mom or Dad stands over the young chicks to keep them dry when it rains!

FLEDGLING The young leave the nest to perch on nearby branches and exercise their wings at 3 weeks of age, but return to the nest for meals. The next week they dine out, and in yet another week or so they fly.

JUVENILE Once they leave the nest, juveniles go out to feeding areas during the day and return to the colony at night to roost.

Did You Know?

The Migratory Bird Treaty Act protects all migratory birds (and any part of the bird) wherever they spend their time. In addition, laws protect all wild birds with the exception of the Rock Pigeon, European Starling and House Sparrow. You may not collect bird feathers, nests, or eggs. You can keep the memory of what you find with a photograph, drawing or painting and by keeping notes in Journal Pages (pages 188-189) for safe wildlife souvenirs.

When

Great Egrets are diurnal. They are active during the day and rest at night.

Migration

Spring Arrival: Mar–Apr
Fall Departure: Aug–Oct
Short- to mid-distance migrant, overwintering in Alabama, Louisiana, Texas and south to Honduras.

Nesting

Begin nesting in April–May in the Northeastern US. Great Egrets nest on their own or in colonies with Snowy Egrets, Great Blue Herons, Little Blue Herons, Black-crowned Night Herons and Glossy Ibises.

Getting Around

Great Egrets move gracefully in flight with their neck tucked in an "S" shape and their black legs trailing behind! They will wade slowly during the day in water up to their belly, looking for small fish and crustaceans to eat.

Where to Look

Great Egrets are found near river floodplains, estuaries, wetlands, streams and shores of shallow bodies of water with open vegetation.

Year-round   Summer
Migration   Winter

Bald Eagle

Haliaeetus leucocephalus

Length: 28–38 inches (71–96 cm)
Wingspan: 6½ feet (204 cm)

adult feeding juvenile

fishing

Large, yellow hooked beak for tearing apart prey

Dark brown-black with a white head

Females and males look the same; females are often larger than males.

"Kwit kwit kwit kwit, kee-kee-kee-kee-ker!" This is fair warning to "Stay out of my territory!"

Large yellow legs and feet with curved talons for capturing and carrying prey

White tail

National Symbol of the USA

The Northeast, with its many lakes, rivers and coasts, is home to an important breeding population of Bald Eagles. However, in 1963 there were only 800 nesting pairs in the lower 48 states. Thanks to regulation, the banning of DDT, and restoration efforts, the population has been downlisted from federally endangered to threatened. To continue to nest successfully in the Northeast, Bald Eagles need tall trees, open water within one mile of the nest, food, roosting areas, and to not be disturbed. With more buildings placed near the water's edge, habitat is lost. You can be part of the Bald Eagle's success story by making choices that consider the needs of this fascinating wild bird of prey!

Habitat Café

Yumm . . . bring an order of fish caught at the water's surface, carrion (dead meat) and water birds including gulls and ducks. Bald Eagles are carnivorous. Eagles can eat large amounts of food and store it in their crop to digest over several days.

SPRING, SUMMER, FALL, WINTER MENU:

 Mostly fish, some birds and a few mammals and reptiles

Life Cycle

NEST Both parents build the nest, or eyrie, in the top of a large tree (cottonwood, red or white pine). The nest is a deep pile of large branches and sticks, lined with smaller twigs, grass, moss and weeds.

EGGS About 3 inches long. Both the female and male incubate the clutch of 2 eggs for 34–36 days.

MOM! DAD! Altricial. Covered with down for the first 5–6 weeks. Parents bring fresh food. The first chick to hatch is generally larger and may kill or starve the second, smaller chick.

NESTLING Feathers grow in at 5 weeks of age but young stay in the nest for 8–14 weeks. Before leaving the nest they practice flapping and landing skills. Half of all nest takeoffs fall short, leaving the bird on the ground, vulnerable to predators. Mom and Dad come to the rescue and bring food until it can fly.

FLEDGLING Fledge at 3–4 months of age.

JUVENILE Juveniles gain their full adult plumage at 5 years of age. They stay with the same mate for life and remain in the same nesting territory each breeding season.

History Hangout

The National Emblem Law of 1940 made it illegal to kill any Bald Eagle in the lower 48 states. They are also protected under the Migratory Bird Treaty Act and are listed as a federally threatened species. Celebrate the Bald Eagle and other wildlife with kids from all over our nation by joining in the activities of National Wildlife Week sponsored by the National Wildlife Federation, http://www.nwf.org/nationalwildlifeweek/. You can celebrate eagles with a wild song too, www.birdsforkids.com.

When

Bald Eagles are diurnal, active during the day and resting at night.

Migration

Spring Arrival: Mar–Apr
Fall Departure: Sep–Nov
Permanent resident to short-distance migrant. Some stay in the Northeastern US all winter along open waters, while others migrate to states to the south. Overwintering eagles group up and need habitat with roosting trees near open-water feeding areas.

Nesting

Bald Eagles begin egg laying and incubation from late February to April in the Northeastern US.

Getting Around

Bald Eagles use their powerful, broad wings to climb, soar and glide.

Where to Look

Bald Eagles can be found region wide with the greatest numbers in areas along lakes, rivers and coasts.

Year-round   Summer
Migration   Winter

Great Blue Heron

Ardea herodias

Length: 38–54 inches (97–137 cm)
Wingspan: 5½–6½ feet (167–201 cm)

in flight

Feather plume

Yellow bill

Adults have a white crown
and black areas on their
wing (shoulders)

Blue-gray with
a white throat
and head

Male and female
look alike

"Rok-rok"
means
"This is my space!"

Rok-Rok, Rookeries

Great Blue Herons nest throughout the Northeastern US in colonies of often 100 or more birds, called rookeries. Some heron rookeries are located along large rivers and forested islands. Going in or near heron colonies during nesting is not a good idea. You might cause the herons to abandon their young. Besides, a heron colony is a very smelly place. Many birds together can create a lot of droppings! Heron colonies are best enjoyed at a distance. Herons may fly out to feeding areas in wetlands over 30 miles from a colony. They are much easier to find and watch as they slowly stalk shoreline shallows in search of fish and other prey.

Habitat Café

Today's Special
snakes

Yumm . . . bring an order of fish, frogs, crayfish, lizards, grasshoppers, mice and shrews. Herons grip or spear prey with their 6-inch pointed bill. Great Blue Herons are carnivorous. They eat only animal matter.

SPRING, SUMMER, FALL, WINTER MENU:
Lots of fish, with fewer insects, reptiles and amphibians

Life Cycle

NEST Hundreds of Great Blue Herons nest together in the tops of tall trees in a colony called a rookery. The nest is built of large sticks. Herons will use the same rookery for many years. Some heron rookeries have been used for nearly 100 years!

EGGS About 2½ inches long. Both the female and male incubate the clutch of 4 eggs for 28 days.

MOM! DAD! Altricial. Both help feed the young.

NESTLING The chicks stay in the nest for about 7–8 weeks.

FLEDGLING They are about the same size as their parents when they leave the nest. The parents continue to feed them for 2–3 weeks.

JUVENILE The juveniles join with others their age, feeding and preparing for migration. They have a black crown, but it takes 2 years to grow a full feather plume. At 3 years they are mature enough to nest and raise young.

Gross Factor

Parents catch, eat and partially digest fish, frogs and other small animals, and deliver the baby food by spitting it up into the chick's open beak. As chicks grow, they take the food out of the parent's beak. Finally, the parents spit the food into the nest and the older chicks fight over the juiciest pieces. Chicks ward off threats from below by leaning over the nest and spitting half-digested fish on the intruder. Gross!

When

Great Blue Herons are diurnal, feeding during the day and resting at night.

Migration

Spring Arrival: Feb–Apr
Fall Departure: Sep–Oct
Short- to mid-distance migrant to the southeastern US and as far south as Panama. Some overwinter along the Atlantic Coast and ice-free waters inland.

Nesting

Great Blue Herons begin to nest in April–June in the Northeastern US.

Getting Around

Herons wade in shallow water, and sometimes stalk on dry land. Their toes spread out as they step on the ground, leaving tracks in the mud 6–8 inches long and 4–6 inches wide. Herons fly with slow, deep, steady wingbeats, legs stretched out behind, and their neck bent into a tight "S" shape.

Where to Look

Great Blue Herons can be found near rivers, streams, coastal and inland wetlands and lakes throughout the Northeastern US.

| Year-round | Summer |
| Migration | Winter |

YOU MIGHT INCLUDE:
- size, shape, field marks
- type of bill and feet
- shape of wings and tail
- feather color and pattern

Sample Journal Entry

Today I was looking in my binoculars and I saw a female robin feeding her chicks. They were in my neighbor's tree on 5/13/10. The chicks were small and gray. They had bright yellow beaks. The female was brown with an orange belly, feet and beak. Her nest was made of sticks and twigs. She was very cool.

OTHER NOTES YOU MAY WANT TO INCLUDE:

- Date, time and habitat
- What the bird was doing (behavior)
- Song/call
- Alone, pair or group of birds

- Flight pattern
- Other signs, like tracks, scat (droppings), nests, eggs, wood chips, wing marks in snow, ice crystals from a snow burrow

Let's start a journal to record your adventures as an outdoor detective!

SEE HOW MANY BIRDS YOU CAN FIND

COPY THIS PAGE FOR MORE JOURNALING

Glossary

Brainy Bird Words and Their Meanings

adaptation A physical feature, behavior, or trait that a bird has developed to help it take full advantage of its habitat. American Robins are found all over the Northeast because they have adapted to a variety of habitats for shelter, nesting and raising their young. They have also adapted to eating a variety of foods. A robin's diet includes worms, insects, seeds, berries and fruits. These meals can be found in rural, city, or suburban habitats around the state.

altricial Baby birds that hatch from the egg helpless. They are naked, unable to see, walk, hop, fly, or feed themselves, and need to be cared for by one or both parents.

anting Some birds, such as the Blue Jay, will place ants between their skin and their feathers with their beak. At times, some birds actually stand on an anthill and allow the ants to crawl up into their feathers!

binomial nomenclature A system of classifying and giving scientific names to plants and animals based on similar identifying characteristics. It is used to group birds together by which body characteristics they have in common. Scientific names originate in Latin and Greek and remain the same all over the world. The scientific name for the American Robin is *Turdus migratorius*.

boreal migrant Birds that breed in Canada, but come south into the Northeast during some years when their northern food supply is scarce.

bristle feathers Stiff, hair-like feathers made up of a firm central shaft (rachis). They usually grow near the eyes, nostrils and beak opening. Bristle feathers may protect the eyes from insects, dust and dirt, or help the bird funnel food into its mouth.

brood patch A bare spot on the chest or belly of a parent bird that is used to incubate eggs. The feathers in this area either fall off or are plucked out. Blood vessels next to the brood patch help keep the eggs warm. In most bird species, feathers regrow after the nesting season.

camouflage A bird's shape, or the color and pattern of its feathers (plumage), that helps it hide from predators or prey. The American Woodcock's plumage is similar in color and pattern to the brown leaves of the deciduous forest where it lives.

coniferous trees Trees that bear their seeds in a cone.

contour feathers These feathers overlap each other to give birds a streamlined body shape (a contour) for less friction. This helps birds fly faster through the air and dive faster in the water. Contour feathers are found on the body, wings and tail. They have a central shaft (rachis) with vanes on each side. Attached to the vanes are barbs. On each side of the barbs are small barbules that make a "zipper" to hold the feather barbs together. When the barbs unzip, the bird uses its beak to zip them back together while preening.

courtship behavior The actions that a bird does to attract a mate. Some birds stomp the ground and turn in circles in a courtship dance. Others perform amazing aerial dances, and some drum on hollow trees. Courtship is the "dating" behavior of birds.

crepuscular Active during the twilight hours, which include the hours of dawn just before the sun rises, and dusk just after the sun sets. Crepuscular birds are active during the time between day and night when the faint light of sunrise and sunset provides them with protection from predators. American Woodcocks are mostly crepuscular.

deciduous forest A forest with trees that lose all their leaves each year. Sugar and red maples, white ash, American beech, northern red oak and black cherry are all deciduous trees.

diurnal Active during the daytime, or the hours that the sun is up. Diurnal birds feed, build their nests and preen during the day. American Robins are diurnal birds.

down feathers These feathers do not "zip" together like contour feathers, but stay fluffy. The air spaces hold the bird's body heat close like a warm blanket. Young birds often have down first to keep their small bodies warm until their contour and other body feathers grow in. Adult birds' down feathers are located under their contour feathers.

egg tooth A newly hatched chick has an egg tooth. This small, sharp projection on its upper mandible (bill) helps it to chip through the egg's shell during hatching. The egg tooth is no longer needed after hatching and soon falls off.

field marks Each bird species has physical features that make it unique (one of a kind). These unique features can help you to identify it. Field marks include feather color, feather pattern, a bird's basic body shape and size. Other field marks include the shape and size of the bird's bill, feet, wings and tail. An eye-ring (which gives the bird the appearance of wearing a pair of glasses) or a crest on the top of its head are also field marks.

fledgling Young birds that have just learned to fly on their own and have left the family nest are called fledglings. To fledge is to be fully feathered and be able to sustain flight.

filoplume feather Delicate, hair-like feathers that help a bird adjust the position of its contour feathers for better flight. Filoplume feathers are scattered over a bird's body. They are sensitive enough to move with the slightest breeze, and send information to nerve cells at their bases.

foraging Gathering food.

game wildlife Birds and other wildlife that can be legally hunted under the laws of the Northeast during designated times of the year. Hunting seasons and limits are specific to each species.

glean To collect or pick up, often referring to gathering food. When a bird picks insect larvae from cracks in tree bark, or spilled grain from a harvested farm field, it is said to be "gleaning."

habitat The place where a bird lives. For a Mallard, home is a shallow lake or wetland habitat where it can reach for the plants and animals on the lake or wetland bottom with its long neck and bill. For a Pileated Woodpecker, home is in a forest habitat with trees big enough for it to make large nesting and roosting holes.

hawking The act of catching insects where the bird sits very still on a perch until it sees a flying insect. It flies out, snatches the insect in mid-air and then returns to the perch to devour the insect or deliver it to its young.

juvenile A young bird that has grown to be independent of its parents (it can fly and find food, water and shelter on its own) but is not yet mature enough to breed. Many smaller birds pass through this stage in their first year; larger birds can remain a juvenile for four or five years. They are the adolescents and teenagers of the bird world.

lift This is what allows a bird to defy gravity and get off the ground. Lift is made by the force of the air pressure underneath the wings, which is greater than the air pressure above the wings, and results in a raising force. The shape of a bird's wings is what makes this work. The top side of the wing is convex (curved), and the bottom is flatter. The air rushing past the wing is divided in two flows: one over the top of the wing and the other past the bottom of the wing. The top air moves faster. This causes the air beneath the wing to go slower and increases the air pressure under the wing—the bird is lifted off the ground. The Swiss scientist **Daniel Bernoulli** (1700–1782) discovered this principle of flight, which is now called **Bernoulli's Principle**.

migration The seasonal movement of birds or animals from one region to another. Bobolinks migrate to wintering grounds in South America in the fall and return to the Northeastern US the following spring to nest and raise their young.

molt When a bird sheds its old feathers and grows new ones to replace them.

navigation How a bird finds its way, such as during migration.

neotropical migrant A bird that breeds in the Northeastern US, but migrates to wintering areas in Central and South America. Includes both mid-distance Central American and long-distance South American migrants.

nocturnal Active during the night. Birds that are nocturnal are active feeding, nest building and preening during the night. Great Horned Owls are nocturnal birds.

nongame wildlife Birds and animals protected by state or national laws from trapping and hunting. Most birds in this book are nongame birds. There is no designated time or "season" to legally hunt them. Game birds, however, can be legally hunted.

ornithology The study of birds. The segment "ology" in a word means the study of, and "ornith" is associated with birds. An ornithologist is a scientist who studies birds.

overwinter To spend the winter. Some Northern Flickers overwinter in the Northeastern US.

permanent resident Birds that breed and remain in the Northeastern US all year. Black-capped Chickadees and Blue Jays are permanent residents in the Northeastern US.

phenology The study of the changing seasons.

plumage A bird's plumage refers to all of its feathers together.

precocial Chicks that hatch able to see, walk, hop, or fly and feed themselves. They need only limited care by one or both parents. The role of the parents in precocial birds is usually to lead the young to food, offer protection from predators, and provide brooding in weather and temperature extremes. The young of many ground-nesting birds such as the Killdeer and Canada Goose are precocial.

predator A bird or animal that captures other living creatures to eat. A Cooper's Hawk is a predator of small mammals that it catches for lunch.

preening When a bird arranges, cleans, fluffs and straightens its feathers.

prey A bird or animal that is captured and eaten by a predator. The small mammals captured for lunch by a Cooper's Hawk are considered its prey.

semiplume feather A combination of a contour feather and a down feather. It has a stiff shaft and soft down vanes that serve as extra insulation to keep a bird warm.

short-distance migrant A bird that breeds in the Northeastern US but winters just far enough south to avoid extreme temperatures and snowfall.

super adaptor A bird that is able to live in a variety of habitats.

syrinx The vocal organ of a bird similar to the larynx (voice box) in humans. Birds use the syrinx to call and sing.

territory A bird's territory is the space that it defends from other birds (and sometimes mammals such as squirrels) for feeding, courtship, nesting and raising its young.

undulating To move in waves, in an up-and-down way.

uropygium gland A gland located above a bird's tail that holds oil. The bird squeezes the gland with its bill to get the oil and then spreads the oil onto its feathers for conditioning.

warm-blooded All birds are warm-blooded. They can keep a constant body temperature no matter how hot or cold the weather. Mammals like you are also warm-blooded. Reptiles and amphibians are cold-blooded. They take on the temperature of their surroundings.

webbed feet When a bird's toes are connected to one another by thick skin, the bird is said to have webbed feet. Mallards and Canada Geese have webbed feet that help them paddle through the water.

wetlands Areas of land that hold water in their soils or are covered with water during all or part of the year. Wetlands can be found separate from other bodies of water, or associated with the shallow edges of a river or lake. Bogs are a special kind of wetland that are very acidic and have a buildup of peat. Plants and animals living in wetland habitats have special adaptations to make the most of the watery conditions.

Do the Math Answer Key

Do the math on your own first and then check if the answer is figured correctly. If not, review the equations in this answer key to find where you worked the math differently. Use your brain power, you can do it!

Ruby-throated Hummingbird

This solution is based on the weight of a 100 pound person. Put your weight in and rework the problem.

Step #1:   Change the percent to a decimal

30% = 3<u>0.</u> = .30

Step #2:   .30 X 100 pounds of body weight = 30 pounds of nectar

Ruffed Grouse

From -27° at the snow's surface to +24° seven inches under the snow = 51 degrees of difference between the temperature at the surface of the snow and the temperature seven inches under the snow. Wow, snow is an efficient insulator.

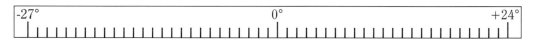

American Robin

14 feet of earthworms per day x 7 days = A robin can eat 98 feet of earthworms in one week! Line up 98 feet of gummy worms, pipe cleaners or string on your sidewalk or driveway to see this amazing feat for yourself.

Cooper's Hawk

66 prey X 3 chicks = 198 prey needed to feed 3 young hawks for six weeks

66 prey X 4 chicks = 264 prey needed to feed 4 young hawks for six weeks

66 prey X 5 chicks = 330 prey needed to feed 5 young hawks for six weeks

Pileated Woodpecker

15 drumbeats in one second X 60 seconds = 900 drumbeats in one minute

900 drumbeats in one minute X 10 minutes = 9000 drumbeats in ten minutes

Red-winged Blackbird

This solution is based on a birth weight of 8 pounds. Place your birth weight in and rework the problem.

8 pounds birth weight X 10 = a weight of 80 pounds in just 10 days

Barn Swallow

Wing loading is the ratio of a bird's wing area to its body weight, or how much "load" each unit area of wing must carry. Birds have different ratios depending on their need for flight in obtaining food, if they migrate, and adaptations to other habitat conditions.

Formula for determining wing load: Bird Weight ÷ Wing Area = WING LOADING

Divide the bird's weight by the total surface area of both wings to find the wing load in pounds per square inch of wing.

.60 ounce of bird weight ÷ 18 square inches of wing area = .03 pounds per square inch of wing

Is it generally true that the larger the bird, the heavier the wing load? Do the math to answer this loaded question!

Ruby-throated Hummingbird

.11 ounce of bird weight ÷ 2 square inches of wing area = _____ pounds per square inch of wing

Mourning Dove

4.6 ounces of bird weight ÷ 55 square inches of wing area = _____ pounds per square inch of wing

Peregrine Falcon

43 ounces of bird weight ÷ 208 square inches of wing area = _____ pounds per square inch of wing

Common Loon

85 ounces of bird weight ÷ 210 square inches of wing area = _____ pounds per square inch of wing

Canada Goose

199 ounces of bird weight ÷ 437 square inches of wing area = _____ pounds per square inch of wing

Did you find a pattern in the numbers that would support the premise that the larger the bird the heavier the wing load?

Wildlife Near and Far: Where to Find Birds

The following state and national resources are great places to learn where bird species may be observed, including nature and environmental centers. Be a citizen scientist and send your observations in to state and national databases listed on these pages.

State Resources

CONNECTICUT
Connecticut Department of Environmental Protection:
http://www.ct.gov/dep/cwp/view.asp?a=2723&q=325726&depNav_GID=1655&depNav=|
http://www.ct.gov/dep/
Connecticut Ornithological Association:
http://www.ctbirding.org/

DELAWARE
Delaware Department of Natural Resources and Environmental Control:
http://www.dnrec.delaware.gov/Pages/default.aspx
DelMarVa Ornithological Society:
http://www.dosbirds.org/

MAINE
Maine Department of Inland Fisheries and Wildlife:
http://www.maine.gov/ifw/wildlife/
Maine Audubon:
http://www.maineaudubon.org/

MARYLAND
Maryland Department of Natural Resources:
http://www.dnr.state.md.us/
Maryland Ornithological Society:
http://www.mdbirds.org/
DelMarVa Ornithological Society:
http://www.dosbirds.org/

MASSACHUSETTS
Massachusetts Department of Fisheries, Wildlife and Environmental Law Enforcement:
http://www.mass.gov/dfwele/dfw/
Brookline Bird Club:
http://massbird.org/bbc/
Massachusetts Audubon Society:
http://www.massaudubon.org/

NEW HAMPSHIRE
New Hampshire Fish and Game Department:
http://www.wildlife.state.nh.us/Wildlife/nongame_and_endangered_wildlife.htm
http://www.wildlife.state.nh.us/
New Hampshire Audubon:
http://www.nhaudubon.org/

NEW JERSEY
New Jersey Division of Fish, Game and Wildlife:
http://www.state.nj.us/dep/fgw/
New Jersey Audubon Society:
http://www.njaudubon.org/

NEW YORK
New York State Department of Environmental Conservation:
http://www.dec.ny.gov/23.html
New York State Ornithological Federation:
http://www.nybirds.org/

PENNSYLVANIA
Pennsylvania Department of Conservation and Natural Resources:
http://www.dcnr.state.pa.us/
Pennsylvania Society for Ornithology:
http://www.pabirds.org/
Delaware Valley Ornithological Club:
http://www.dvoc.org/Main.htm

RHODE ISLAND
Rhode Island Department of Environmental Management:
http://www.dem.ri.gov/programs/bnatres/fishwild/index.htm

VERMONT
Vermont Agency of Natural Resources:
http://www.anr.state.vt.us/

Citizen Science Resources

Birds for Kids:
www.birdsforkids.com

Christmas/Holiday Bird Count:
www.audubon.org/bird/cbc/index.html

Great Backyard Bird Count:
www.birdsource.org/gbbcApps/kids

International Migratory Bird Day:
http://www.birdday.org/

Cornell Lab: Macaulay Library of Sounds:
http://macaulaylibrary.org/index.do

National Bird Feeding Society:
http://www.birdfeeding.org/

National Wildlife Federation:
National Wildlife Week:
http://www.nwf.org/Get-Outside/Be-Out-There/
EventsNational-Wildlife-Week.aspx

The Nature Conservancy:
http://www.nature.org/tncscience/?src=l10

North American Bluebird Society:
http://www.nabluebirdsociety.org/

North American Breeding Bird Survey:
http://www.pwrc.usgs.gov/BBS/

Cornell Lab of Ornithology:
http://www.birds.cornell.edu/

Partners in Flight:
http://www.partnersinflight.org/

Project Feeder Watch:
www.birds.cornell.edu/pfw/

Project Pigeon Watch:
www.birds.cornell.edu/pigeonwatch

US Fish & Wildlife Service:
http://www.fws.gov/educators/E_birds.html

Wild About Science:
http://www.wildaboutscience.net

National Resources

American Birding Association:
Birding Trails:
http://www.aba.org/resources/birdingtrails.html
Birding Festivals:
http://www.aba.org/festivals/index.php

National Audubon Society:
General Information:
http://www.audubon.org/
Birding Trails:
http://www.audubon.org/bird_trails/backseat_birder.html

Important Bird Areas:
http://www.audubon.org/bird/iba/

National Wildlife Federation:
http://www.nwf.org/naturefind/

Watchable Wildlife:
http://www.wildlifeviewingareas.com/

Also visit the websites for your local, state and national parks and forests

Birding Trails in the Northeastern US

Hit the trails and get to know the birds in this book first-hand. There are many birding trails throughout the region, but there is only space to list the main trails here. Explore them all, big and small!

· The Connecticut Coastal Birding Trail
· The Connecticut River Birding Trail
· Delaware Birding Trail
· Maine Birding Trail
· Massachusetts Birding Trails
· New Jersey Birding and Wildlife Trails
· The Lake Champlain Birding Trail
· Audubon Niagara Birding Trail
· Susquehanna River, Eastern PA, Western PA Birding and Wildlife Trails
· Birding Trail updates: www.birdtrail.org

Bird Species by Taxonomic Order

This taxonomic list draws from the common Linnean system, which classifies birds and other living things by their morphological (physical) features. It was developed over two hundred years ago by Carl Linnaeus, a Swedish naturalist. Learn more about scientific names on page 13, in "What's In a Name? Binomial Nomenclature."

ANSERIFORMES: DUCKS, GEESE, SWANS, WATERFOWL
- Canada Goose
- Wood Duck
- Mallard
- Hooded Merganser

GALLIFORMES: CHICKENS, QUAIL, TURKEYS, PHEASANTS
- Northern Bobwhite
- Ruffed Grouse
- Wild Turkey

GAVIIFORMES: LOONS
- Common Loon

PODICIPEDIFORMES: GREBES
- Pied-billed Grebe

CICONIIFORMES: HERONS, BITTERNS, EGRETS
- Great Blue Heron
- Great Egret

FALCONIFORMES: EAGLES, HAWKS, FALCONS
- Osprey
- Bald Eagle
- Northern Harrier
- Cooper's Hawk
- Red-tailed Hawk
- American Kestrel
- Peregrine Falcon

CHARADRIIFORMES: SHOREBIRDS, GULLS, TERNS, PLOVERS, SANDPIPERS
- Piping Plover
- Killdeer
- American Oystercatcher
- Spotted Sandpiper
- American Woodcock
- Ring-billed Gull

COLUMBIFORMES: DOVES, PIGEONS
- Mourning Dove

STRIGIFORMES: OWLS
- Eastern Screech-Owl
- Great Horned Owl
- Snowy Owl
- Barred Owl

APODIFORMES: HUMMINGBIRDS, SWIFTS
- Chimney Swift
- Ruby-throated Hummingbird

CORACIIFORMES: KINGFISHERS
- Belted Kingfisher

PICIFORMES: WOODPECKERS
- Yellow-bellied Sapsucker
- Downy Woodpecker
- Northern Flicker
- Pileated Woodpecker

PASSERIFORMES: PERCHINGS BIRDS, SONGBIRDS
- Eastern Phoebe
- Eastern Kingbird
- Red-eyed Vireo
- Gray Jay
- Blue Jay
- Common Raven
- Barn Swallow
- Black-capped Chickadee
- Boreal Chickadee
- Red-breasted Nuthatch
- White-breasted Nuthatch
- Brown Creeper
- House Wren
- Marsh Wren
- Eastern Bluebird
- American Robin
- Gray Catbird
- Brown Thrasher
- Ovenbird
- Common Yellowthroat
- Savannah Sparrow
- Song Sparrow
- White-throated Sparrow
- Dark-eyed Junco
- Northern Cardinal
- Rose-breasted Grosbeak
- Indigo Bunting
- Bobolink
- Red-winged Blackbird
- Eastern Meadowlark
- Brown-headed Cowbird
- Baltimore Oriole
- Purple Finch
- American Goldfinch

This order follows the most recent version accepted by the American Ornithologists' Union, recently revised to include DNA evidence.

Index

References

The resources used to prepare this book include numerous reports and surveys, many from state breeding bird atlases, the Important Bird Areas Program (IBA) of The National Audubon Society and state Wildlife Action Plans including the data associated with identified Species of Greatest Conservation Need. A complete reference list can be found at Adele Porter's author website: www.adeleporter.com. General references and sources of additional information include the following books, reports, and publications:

Gill, F., and Poole, A., eds. *The Birds of North America, volumes 1–18*. Philadelphia: Academy of Natural Sciences; Washington, D.C.: American Ornithologists' Union; Ithaca: Cornell Lab of Ornithology, 2002.

Lynch, Patrick J., and Proctor, Noble S. *Manual of Ornithology, Avian Structure and Function*. New Haven: Yale University Press, 1993.

Partners in Flight. North American Landbird Conservation Plan, 2005. http://www.partnersinflight.org/cont_plan/PIF3_Part2WEB.pdf

Perrins C.M., ed. *Oxford Ornithology Series*. New York: Oxford University Press, 2002.

Podulka, S., Rohrbaugh, R.W. Jr., Bonny, R., eds. *Handbook of Bird Biology, Second Edition*. Ithaca: Cornell Lab of Ornithology; Princeton: Princeton University Press, 2004.

Poole, A., ed. *The Birds of North America Online*: http://bna.birds.cornell.edu/BNA/. Ithaca: Cornell Laboratory of Ornithology, 2005.

Raymo, Chet, and Raymo, Maureen E. *Written in Stone: A Geological History of the Northeastern US., 3rd Edition*. Hensonville: Black Dome Press, 2001.

Sauer, J. R., Hines, J. E., Fallon, J. eds. *The North American Breeding Bird Survey, Results and Analysis 1966–2007. Version 5.15.2008*. Laurel: USGS Patuxent Wildlife Research Center, 2008.

About the Author

Award-winning author and science educator Adele Porter combines her passion for science and dedication to children in her new books. In fact, the students that Adele has worked with during 20 years as an educator inspired *Wild About Northeastern Birds*. Adele has also written educational materials for the Minnesota Department of Natural Resources, the US Forest Service and various publications. She is a member of the National Science Teachers' Association, the American Ornithologists' Union, and the Society of Children's Book Writers and Illustrators.

For Adele, one of the best parts of being an author is meeting the readers of her books at author programs and book signings and hearing their enthusiastic outdoor adventure stories. She looks forward to hearing of your new wildlife adventures!

A native of Minnesota, Adele enjoys the time she and her three children spend together more than anything else. She can be contacted via her author website, www.adeleporter.com.

Go to www.birdsforkids.com to download and print a free bookmark that features a life-size Black-capped Chickadee and tells how to use your book to identify a bird!